PRABHUI _____

AND THE

JALADUTA

INCARNATIONS

"**Today I have disclosed my mind to my companion Lord Sri Krishna.** There is a Bengali poem made by me today in this connection. At about eleven there is a little lurching. **The captain tells that they had never such calmness of the Atlantic. I said it is Lord Krishna's mercy.** His wife asked me to come back again with them so that they may have again a calm Atlantic Ocean. **If Atlantic would have shown its usual face perhaps I would have died. But Lord Krishna has taken charge of the ship.**"

Srila Prabhupada's Jaladuta Diary
Monday 13th and Tuesday 14th September 1965

PRABHUPADA AND THE JALADUTA INCARNATIONS

By Mukunda dasa

Cover Design by Mukunda dasa (Mark Whiteley)

First edition published April 2023

For more information visit:

http://prabhupada.org.uk/

https://truth.prabhupada.org.uk/

https://sulocana-dasa.prabhupada-krishna.co.uk/

Contact: mukunda.dasa@prabhupada.org.uk

Dedicated To Srila Prabhupada

"So although a physical body is not present,
the vibration should be accepted as the presence
of the spiritual master, vibration. What we have
heard from the spiritual master, that is living."

Prabhupada Lecture, 13/1/69, Los Angeles.

In Loving Memory of

Indira Devi Dasi

10/04/1972 - 24/06/2022

"The Lord did not appear before Srila Prabhupada because of Prabhupada's imagination. No, the Supreme Personality of Godhead directly appeared in His many forms of incarnation, saved His pure devotee and took direct charge of the Jaladuta rowing the boat to America. Thus the Lord fulfilled Prabhupada's desire to execute the order of Sri Srimad Bhaktisiddhanta Sarasvati Thakur."

Mukunda dasa, Chapter Two
It Is All Factual; It Is Not A Dream

Srila Prabhupada in India before leaving for America

Srila Prabhupada in India before leaving for America

On March 10, 1959 the MS Jaladuta was launched at the shipbuilding yard of Flenderwerke AG in Lübeck, Germany. The MS Jaladuta slides off the yard towards the Elbe-Trave Kanal for its first test run. Nice to see the auspicious Swastika in Germany in 1959, although it was outlawed after 1945. Evidently, Krishna made sure that the carrier for His confidential pure devotee was made in Germany to ensure a safe voyage.

The picture above displays Shri Patel of Scindia and a representative of the Flenderwerke shipyard preparing the ceremonial fire.

Shri Patel painting (above) the Swastika on the bow of the vessel.

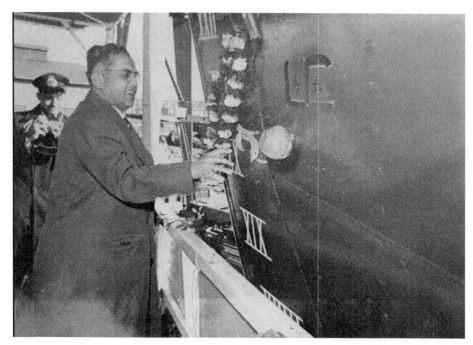

The procedure is that the yard invites a prominent figure to speak the name of the vessel while simultaneously breaking a bottle of champagne over the bow. In this case the shipbuilders invited members of the board of Scindia, and instead of a bottle of alcohol, a blessed coconut was used to inaugurate the name giving ceremony.

In January 1965, Srila Prabhupada left the Radha-Damodara temple in Vrindavan, destined for America, and he didn't return for two years. He printed Volume three of Srimad-Bhagavatam in January, sold them in Bombay in March, and until June 10, 1965, he stayed in Delhi acquiring a passport and sponsorship papers for traveling to the United States. Prabhupada returned to Bombay where he obtained free passage to New York aboard the Scindia Steamship, Jaladuta. Srila Prabhupada had unswerving faith in his guru's order to preach in the English speaking countries. And he had absolute confidence in the unlimited spiritual potency of Lord Krishna's holy names.

The rooms rented by Srila Prabhupada at Radha-Damodara temple. The double doors on the right lead to Srila Prabhupada's kitchen.

Srila Prabhupada's bed in his living room at Radha-Damodara temple.

Inside the kitchen. From its window, Srila Prabhupada
could see the Samadhi of Srila Rupa Gosvami.

By 1965, Bhaktivedanta Swami published the third and final part of the first canto of Srimad- Bhagavatam. One day he met Mr. Agarwal, a Mathura businessman, and mentioned to him in passing, as he did to almost everyone he met, that he wanted to go to the West. Although Mr. Agarwal had known Bhaktivedanta Swami for only a few minutes, he volunteered to get him a sponsor in America.

With Sponsorship papers in hand, Bhaktivedanta Swami went to Bombay and met Sumati Morarji, the head of the Scindia Steamship Line, who had helped him with a large donation for printing Volume Two of Srimad-Bhagavatam. He showed his sponsorship papers to her secretary, Mr. Choksi, who was impressed and went to Mrs. Morarji on his behalf.

"The Swami from Vrindavana is back", he told her. "He has published his book on your donation. He has a sponsor, and he wants to go to America. He wants you to send him on a Scindia ship."

Mrs. Morarji said no, "The Swamiji is too old to go to the United States and accomplish anything."

Mr. Choksi conveyed to him Mrs. Morarji's words, but Bhaktivedanta Swami listened disapprovingly. She wanted him to stay in India and complete Srimad-Bhagavatam. "Why go to the United States?" She had argued. "Finish the job here."

Bhaktivedanta Swami, however, was fixed on going. He told Mr. Choksi that he should convince Mrs. Morarji. He coached Mr. Choksi on what he should say: "I find this gentleman very inspired to go to the States and preach something to the people there ... " But when he told Mrs. Morarji, she again said no. The Swami was not healthy and it would be too cold there. People in America were not so cooperative, and they would probably not listen to him. Exasperated with Mr. Choksi's ineffectiveness, Bhaktivedanta Swami demanded a personal interview. It was granted, and a grey- haired, determined Bhaktivedanta Swami presented his emphatic request, "Please give me one ticket."

Sumati Morarji was concerned. "Swamiji, you are so old-you are taking this responsibility. Do you think it is all right?"

"No," he reassured her, lifting his hand as if to reassure a doubting daughter, "it is all right."

"But do you know what my secretaries think?" said Mrs. Morarji, "They say, 'Swamiji is going to die there.'" Bhaktivedanta made a face as if to dismiss a foolish rumor. Again he insisted that she give him a ticket.

"AII right," she said, "Get your P-form, and I will make an arrangement to send you by our ship."

Bhaktivedanta Swami smiled brilliantly and contently left her offices, past her amazed and skeptical clerks.

Bhaktivedanta Swami, arrived in Calcutta about two weeks before the Jaladuta's departure. Although he had lived much of his life in the city, he now had nowhere to stay. It was as he had written in his "Vrindavana Bhajana": "I have my wife, Sons, daughters, grandsons, everything, But I have no money, so they are a fruitless glory." Although in this city he had been so carefully nurtured as a child, those early days were also gone forever: "Where have my loving father and mother gone to now? And where are all my elders, who were my own folk? Who will give me news of them, tell me who? All that is left of this family life is a list of names."

Out of the hundreds of people in Kolkata whom Bhaktivedanta Swami knew, he chose to call on Mr. Sisir Bhattacarya, the flamboyant kirtana singer he had met a year before at the governor's house in Lucknow. Mr. Bhattacarya was not a relative, not a disciple, nor even a close friend; but he was willing to help. Bhaktivedanta Swami called at his place and informed him that he would be leaving on a cargo ship in a few days; he needed a place to stay, and he would like to give some lectures. Mr. Bhattacarya immediately began to arrange a few private meetings at friends' homes, where he would sing and Bhaktivedanta Swami would then speak.

A week before his departure, on August 6, Bhaktivedanta Swami traveled to Mayapur to visit the Samadhi of Srila Bhaktisiddhanta Sarasvati. "You have ordered me to preach in the west and now after so many years I am going. Please give me your blessings and pray to Krishna to protect me."

As the day of his departure approached, Bhaktivedanta Swami took stock of his meager possessions. He had only suitcase, an umbrella, and a supply of dry cereal. He did not know what he would find to eat in America; perhaps there would be only meat. If so, he was prepared to live on boiled potatoes and the cereal. His main baggage, several trunks of books, was being handled separately by Scindia Cargo. Two hundred three-volume sets-the very thought of the books gave him confidence.

Srila Prabhupada setting outside his room at the Radha Krishna temple at 2439 Chhipiwada Kalan in old Delhi before leaving for America. In front of him are the first three volumes of his English Srimad Bhagavatam.

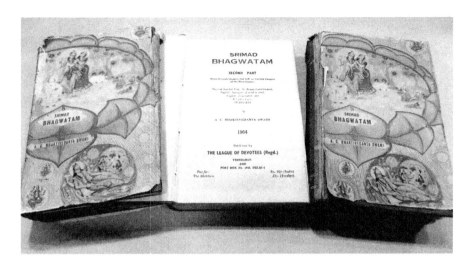

(above) The first three volumes of his English Srimad Bhagavatam.

(left) The front entrance of the temple at 2439 Chhipiwada Kalan, which Srila Prabhupada listed as his residence.

The veranda outside Srila Prabhupada's room at 2439 Chhipiwada Kalan.

The inside of Srila Prabhupada's room. The miniature dome indicates that the Radha-Krishna Deities are situated directly beneath this spot.

Sumati Morarji agreed to let Srila Prabhupada reside at the Scindia Colony, a compound of apartments for Scindia employees, while he was waiting for his departure papers. Srila Prabhupada stayed and did his typing in this room. The furniture is new and was not there at the time of his tenure.

Srila Prabhupada held preaching programs in this room before he left for America. Little has changed since 1965.

(left) The outside veranda of Srila Prabhupada's room.

(below) August 13th 1965 - just a few days before his seventieth birthday Srila mounted the gangway of the Jaladuta

The Jaladuta was a regular cargo carrier of the Scindia Steam Navigation Company, but there was a passenger cabin aboard. During the voyage from Kolkata to New York in August and September of 1965, the cabin was occupied by "Sri Abhay Caranaravinda Bhaktivedanta Swami," whose age was listed as sixty-nine and who was taken on board bearing "a complimentary ticket with food."

The Jaladuta, under the command of Captain Arun Pandia, whose wife was also on board, left at 9:00 a.m. on Friday, August 13, 1965.

Srila Prabhupada : So some way or other, in 1965, I went to America with great difficulty. But I took about two hundred sets of books. The customs clearance was done, I told them that 'Oh, I am taking these books for distribution. Not for sale.' Anyway, they passed, and with these books I reached America.

This newspaper article announcing Śrīla Prabhupāda's departure for the West appeared in the Dainik Basumati, a Bengali newspaper in Calcutta. The translation of the article is as follows:

"The Lord's Message Goes to America

"Lord Śrī Kṛṣṇa Caitanya Mahāprabhu said, pṛthivīte āche yata nagarādi grāma, sarvatra pracāra haibe mora nāma. That prophecy is going to be fulfilled now!

"Śrīmat Bhaktivedanta Swami, a resident of Vṛndāvana, has translated the Śrīmad-Bhāgavatam into English in sixty volumes with word-for-word meaning and purports. Before this great work could be appreciated by his countrymen, people from far off America have expressed their admiration of his supernormal achievement and have invited him so that they may meet him in person and acquaint themselves with his work. Hence he is departing from Calcutta for New York this 12th day of August."

THE SCINDIA STEAM NAVIGATION CO. LTD.
BOMBAY

Nº 774·

Place of issue _Calcutta_ Date _4. 8. 19 65_

CABIN CLASS
NON-TRANSFERABLE PASSAGE TICKET

PER Regular Cargo Carrier s.s. _Jaladuta_ m.v. embarking about _____ 19 ___

From the port of _Calcutta Back_ to the port of _____

Names	AGE Yrs.	Mths.	Cabin No.	Berth No.	Passage Fare	Taxes
1 Sri Abhoy Charan Aravinda Bhaktivedanta Swami	69		1			
2						
3						
4						
5 (Complimentary			Ticket	with	Food)	
6						
7						

Adults _1_   Children _._   Infants _._   TOTAL _one_.

IT IS MUTUALLY AGREED that this contract ticket is issued by or on behalf of THE SCINDIA STEAM NAVIGATION CO. LTD. and is accepted by the passenger(s) on the terms and conditions printed or endorsed on the face and back of this ticket.

For The Scindia Steam Navigation Co. Ltd.

(K. B. Mehta)
Senior Deputy Manager

Srila Prabhupada's Jaladuta Ticket: "So my Guru Maharaja ordered me long, long ago, when I was twenty- five years old, my Guru Maharaja ordered me to go to the foreign countries and preach Lord Caitanya's message. But somehow or other I could not assimilate his order until I was seventy years old.

But it was better late than never. So also I was trying how to make a successful tour for preaching Caitanya Mahaprabhu's message. So by the grace of my Guru Maharaja and by your blessings, I went to the Western countries and had such a very good response, very good response. I went there empty handed with forty rupees in my pocket and free ticket, return ticket, by the Scindia Steam Navigation Company. And for one year I had no place to live, I had no money to eat; still I was going here and there."
Arrival Lecture New Delhi, November 10, 1971

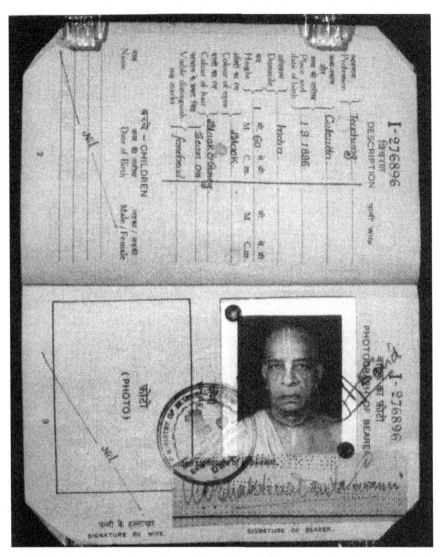

Srila Prabhupada experienced no difficulty in obtaining his passport, and with the help of his friend and sponsor Krishna Pandit, it was issued to him on June 10th.

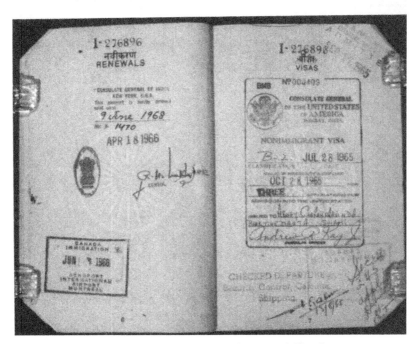

Obtaining the visa, however, proved more difficult. It was not until July 28th, after much endeavor, and with the help of Mr. Choksi from the Scindia Company, that it was finally approved.

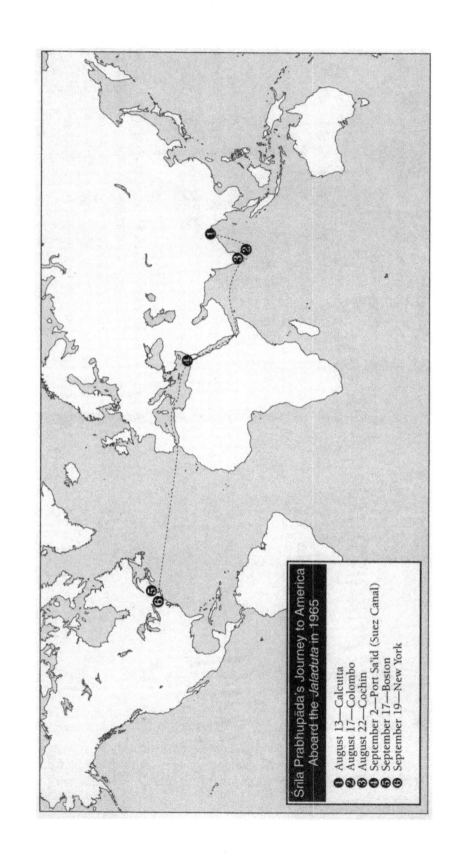

Śrīla Prabhupāda's Journey to America
Aboard the *Jaladuta* in 1965

① August 13—Calcutta
② August 17—Colombo
③ August 22—Cochin
④ September 2—Port Saïd (Suez Canal)
⑤ September 17—Boston
⑥ September 19—New York

The front cover of the diary Srila Prabhupada used on the Jaladuta. He signed his name at the top. On the right is the inside cover of the diary.

SCINDIA

With *Best Compliments of*
THE
SCINDIA STEAM NAVIGATION
COMPANY LIMITED
SCINDIA HOUSE
BALLARD ESTATE BOMBAY - 1

PERSONAL MEMORANDA

NAME *A. C. Bhaktivedanta Swami*

ADDRESS *P.O. Box No 1846*

2439, Chhipiwada Kalan

Delhi 6.

TELEPHONE { OFFICE *Delhi*

RESIDENCE *Vrindaban*

TELEGRAPHIC ADDRESS

CAMERA No

MOTOR CAR No

MOTOR CAR RENEWAL DUE

LIFE INSURANCE POLICY No

PREMIUM DUE

GENERAL *Ry. Pass no 005379*

A. C. Bhaktivedanta Swami

1965

First Class Dining Saloon.

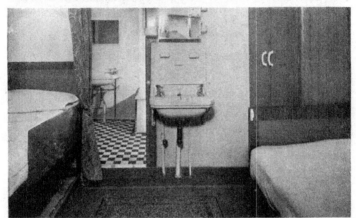

First Class Two-Berth De Luxe Cabin.

First Class Lounge

Inside the Jaladuta.

The Jaladuta leaving port.

The Jaladuta leaving port.

The Jaladuta crossing the ocean.

The Jaladuta crossing the ocean.

The Jaladuta crossing the ocean.

M.V. "JALADUTA" MESSENGER OF THE WATER

On the nineteenth, August, 1965, when the ship arrived at Colombo, Ceylon (now Sri Lanka), Bhaktivedanta Swami was able to get relief from his seasickness. The captain took him ashore, and he traveled around Colombo by car. Then the ship went on toward Cochin, on the west coast of India. Janmastami, the appearance day of Lord Krishna, fell on the twentieth of August that year. Bhaktivedanta Swami took the opportunity to speak to the crew about the philosophy of Lord Krishna, and he distributed prasadam he had cooked himself.

August 21 was his seventieth birthday, observed (without ceremony) at sea. That same day the ship arrived at Cochin, and Bhaktivedanta Swami's trunks of Srimad-Bhagavatam volumes, which had been shipped from Mumbai, were loaded on board.

By the twenty-third the ship had put out to the Red Sea, where Bhaktivedanta Swami encountered great difficulty. He noted in his diary, "Rain, seasickness, dizziness, headache, no appetite, vomiting." The symptoms persisted, but it was more than seasickness. The pains in his chest made him think he would die at any moment. In two days he suffered two heart attacks. He tolerated the difficulty, meditating on the purpose of his mission, but after two days of such violent attacks he thought that if another were to come he would certainly not survive.

On the night of the second day, Bhaktivedanta Swami had a dream. Lord Krishna, in His many forms, was rowing a boat, and He told Bhaktivedanta Swami that he should not fear, but should come along. Bhaktivedanta Swami felt assured of Lord Krishna's protection and the violent attacks did not recur. The Jaladuta entered the Suez Canal on September 1 and stopped in Port Said on the second. Bhaktivedanta Swami visited the city with the captain and said that he liked it. By the sixth he had recovered a little from his illness and was eating regularly again for the first time in two weeks, having cooked his own kichari and puris. He reported in his diary that his strength renewed little by little.

Srila Prabhupada : Thursday, September 9: this afternoon, we have crossed over the Atlantic Ocean for twenty-four hours. The whole day was clear and almost smooth. I am taking my food regularly and have got some strength to struggle. There is also a slight tacking of the ship and I am feeling a slight headache also. But I am struggling and the nectarine of life is Sri Chaitanya Charitamrita, the source of all my vitality.

Friday, September 10 : Today the ship is plying very smoothly. I feel today better. But I am feeling separation from Sri Vrindaban and my Lords Sri Govinda, Gopinath, Radha Damodar. The only solace is Sri Caitanya Caritamrta in which I am tasting the nectar of Lord Caitanya's lila [pastimes] and have left Bharatabhumi just to execute the order of Sri Bhaktisiddhanta Sarasvati in pursuance of Lord Caitanya's order. I have no qualification, but have taken up the risk just to carry out the order of His Divine I depend fully on their mercy, so far away from Vrindaban.

Prabhupada: Hmm. The name is there, he remembered. After all, he is officer. He knows so many things. So it is a great history. (laughs) **There was two days I was attacked in heart on the ship. So hardship.**

Trivikrama: Then you had a dream?

Prabhupada: Hmm.

Hari-sauri: What was that, Srila Prabhupada?

Prabhupada: That is... (laughs) The dream was I must come here.

Hari-sauri: It was some instruction that you got?

Prabhupada: **The dream was that Krishna in His many forms was bowing the row. What is called?**

Hari-sauri: **Rowing the boat.**

Prabhupada: **Yes.**

[Srila Prabhupada Room Conversation, June 8, 1976, Los Angeles]

Sri Caitanya Mahaprabhu, however, wanted to inform us that actually it was not a dream. He actually came there and rowed the boat in His many forms of incarnation. Such are the dealings of Srila Prabhupada with the Supreme Personality of Godhead. The Lord personally talked with Srila Prabhupada, and His Divine Grace also saw Him in His many forms rowing the Jaladuta to America. It was all factual; it was not a dream.

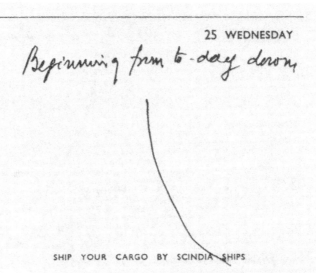

25 WEDNESDAY

Beginning from to-day down,

SHIP YOUR CARGO BY SCINDIA SHIPS

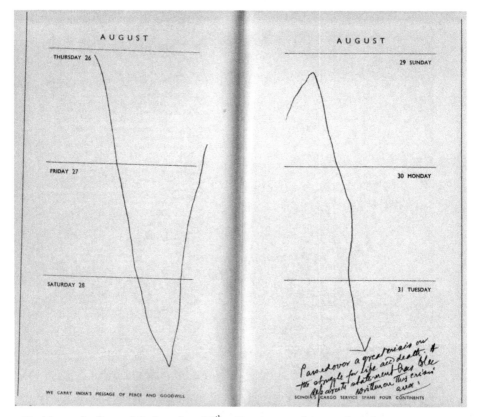

AUGUST

THURSDAY 26

FRIDAY 27

SATURDAY 28

WE CARRY INDIA'S MESSAGE OF PEACE AND GOODWILL

AUGUST

29 SUNDAY

30 MONDAY

31 TUESDAY

Passed over a great crisis on the struggle for life and death. A separate statement has to be written on this crisis area

SCINDIA'S CARGO SERVICE SPANS FOUR CONTINENTS

Prabhupada diary: Wednesday 25th – Beginning from today down.

Tuesday 31st – Passed over a great crisis on the struggle for life and death. A separate statement has to be written on this crisis area.

During the voyage, Bhaktivedanta Swami sometimes stood on deck at the ship's rail, watching the ocean and the sky and thinking of Caitanya-caritamrta, Vrindavana-dhama, and the order of his spiritual master to go preach in the West. Mrs. Pandia, the captain's wife, whom Bhaktivedanta Swami considered to be "an intelligent and learned lady," foretold Bhaktivedanta Swami's future. If he were to pass beyond this crisis in his health, she said, it would indicate the good will of Lord Krishna.

The ocean voyage of 1965 was a calm one for the Jaladuta. The captain said that never in his entire career had he seen such a calm Atlantic crossing. Bhaktivedanta Swami replied that the calmness was Lord Krishna's mercy, and Mrs. Pandia asked Bhaktivedanta Swami to come back with them so that they might have another such crossing. Bhaktivedanta Swami wrote in his diary, "If the Atlantic would have shown its usual face, perhaps I would have died. But Lord Krishna has taken charge of the ship."

After thirty-five-day journey from Kolkata, the Jaladuta reached Boston's Commonwealth Pier at 5:30 A.M. On September 17,1965, the ship was to stop briefly in Boston before proceeding to New York City. Among the first things Bhaktivedanta Swami saw in America were the letters "A & P" painted on a pier front warehouse. The gray waterfront dawn revealed the ships in the harbor, a conglomeration of lobster stands and drab buildings, and, rising in the distance, the Boston skyline.

Srila Prabhupada: So when I was on the ship at Boston port, Commonwealth port, I was thinking that, I have come here. I do not know what is the purpose because, how will the people will accept this movement? They are differently educated, and as soon as I say, 'So, my dear sir, you have to give up meat-eating and illicit sex and no intoxication and gambling,' they will say, 'Please go home.'

The Jaladuta arriving in port.

The Jaladuta arriving in port.

The Jaladuta arriving in port.

Srila Prabhupada goes down the gangway of the
Jaladuta and arrives in America.

I have no devotion, nor do I have any knowledge, but I have
strong faith in the holy name of Krishna. I have been designated
as Bhaktivedanta, and now, if You like, You can fulfill the
real purport of Bhaktivedanta.

Signed-the most unfortunate, insignificant beggar

A.C. Bhaktivedanta Swami,

on board the ship Jaladuta, Commonwealth Pier,
Boston, Massachusetts, U.S.A. Dated 18th of September, 1965

Bhaktivedanta Swami had to pass through U.S. Immigration and Customs in Boston. His visa allowed him a three-month stay, and an official stamped it to indicate his expected date of departure. Captain Pandia invited Bhaktivedanta Swami to take a walk into Boston, where the captain intended to do some shopping. They walked across a footbridge into a busy commercial area with old churches, warehouses, office buildings, bars, tawdry bookshops, nightclubs and restaurants.

On board the ship that day, Bhaktivedanta Swami wrote a poem that he titled, 'Markine Bhagavata-dharma' - Teaching Krishna Consciousness in America. He wrote, "My dear Lord Krishna, You are so kind upon this useless soul, but I do not know why you have brought me here. Now you can do whatever You like with me. But I guess you have some business here, otherwise why would You bring me to this terrible place?"

On the nineteenth of September, the Jaladuta sailed into New York Harbor and docked at a Brooklyn pier, at Seventeenth Street. Bhaktivedanta Swami saw the awesome Manhattan skyline, the Empire State Building, and like millions of visitors and immigrants in the past, the Statue of Liberty. He was dressed appropriately as a resident of Vrindavana. He wore kanthi-mala (neck beads) and a simple cotton dhoti, and he carried japa-mala (chanting beads) and an old chadar, or shawl. His complexion was golden, his head shaven, sikha in the back, his forehead decorated with the whitish Vaishnava tilaka. He wore pointed white rubber slippers, not uncommon for sadhus in India. But who in New York had ever seen or dreamed of anyone appearing like this Vaishnava? He was possibly the first Vaishnava sannyasi to arrive in New York with uncompromised appearance. Of course, New Yorkers have an expertise in not giving much attention to any kind of strange new arrival.

I emphatically say to you, O brothers, you will obtain your
good fortune from the Supreme Lord Krishna only when
Srimati Radharani becomes pleased with you. (Page 89)

(left): "By his strong desire, the holy name of Lord Gauranga will spread
throughout all the countries of the Western world. In all the cities, towns,
and villages on the earth, from all the oceans, seas, rivers,and streams,
everyone will chant the holy name of Krishna."

"As the vast mercy of Sri Caitanya Mahaprabhu conquers all directions, a
flood of transcendental ecstasy will certainly cover the land. When all the
sinful, miserable living entities become happy, the Vaisnavas' desire is then
fulfilled." (Page 89)

"My mission is to revive a people's God consciousness," says the Swamiji." The Butler Eagle ran an article on Srila Prabhupada just three days after his arrival in the U.S.A., designating him "Ambassador of Bhakti-yoga."

The mind of the pure devotee is always fixed firmly upon the lotus feet of the Lord, the Supreme Personality of Godhead, Sri Krishna, who appears in the land of Vrindavan as a simple cowherd boy yet is the cause of all causes.

Srila Prabhupada first landed here, at commonwealth Pier in Boston, at 5.30 a.m. on September 17th, 1965. This picture was taken in 1968, when Srila Prabhupada revisited the site with some of his disciples

Srila Prabhupada at a speaking engagement in the early 70's with Sumati Morarji, the proprietor of the Scindia Steam Navigation Company. Srila Prabhupada wrote a letter to her after his arrival in America. (See appendix 4 on page 151)

TABLE OF CONTENTS

Glorify The Spiritual Master By His Activities

When we offer respect to the spiritual master or anyone, we glorify his transcendental qualities. That is glorification. Just like we offer respect to Krishna, glorify Him. So this is very important process, glorify the spiritual master by his activities, what he is actually doing. That is glorification. *[Srimad-Bhagavatam Lecture 1.2.3 Rome, May 27, 1974]*

My main purpose for compiling this book is to establish in the devotee community of the whole world, the worship of Srila Prabhupada and the Jaladuta Incarnations. This transcendental pastime should be celebrated as a yearly festival by all devotees of the Lord.

This divine lila of Srila Prabhupada with the Lord reveals to us very clearly the exalted personality of His Divine Grace and the importance of his great mission of spreading love of Krishna to all the fallen conditioned souls.

Prabhupada's position in the ten thousand year Golden Age now unfolding on this planet is so pivotal that the Lord personally incarnated in multiple transcendental forms to protect and carry him on the Jaladuta to America.

Those who are serving the Lord under the direct shelter of Srila Prabhupada and are glorifying this transcendental pastime are also protected by the Jaladuta Incarnations.

In these very difficult times we are all harassed by the ruling principles of Hiranyakasipu.* I therefore pray that the publication of this book which glorifies this wonderous Jaladuta pastime, goes out into the ether like the sound from a transcendental conchshell and shatters the hearts of these demons thus giving faith and joy to all pious souls.

Param vijayate sri-krsna-sankirtanam

Let there be all victory for the chanting of the holy name of Lord Krishna.

Mukunda dasa.

26/01/23

* Disturbances similar to those created by Hiranyakasipu (a great demon from history who terrorized the universe) are now taking place all over the world because of demoniac governments. As stated in the Twelfth Canto of Srimad-Bhagavatam, the men of the governments of Kali-yuga will be no better than rogues and plunderers. Thus the populace will be harassed on one side by scarcity of food and on another by heavy taxation by the government. In other words, the people in most parts of the world in this age are harassed by the ruling principles of Hiranyakasipu. *[Prabhupada from Srimad Bhagavatam 7.8.47]*

The Neglected Transcendental Pastime

It is now over 57 years since Srila Prabhupada's historic and earth changing journey on the ship appropriately named the Jaladuta. [Jala means water or ocean and Duta means the messenger]. The following is taken from the introduction to the Jaladuta Diary:

> Srila Prabhupada was instructed by his spiritual master, Srila Bhaktisiddhanta Sarasvati Thakura, to preach Krishna consciousness to the English-speaking peoples. Toward this end, His Divine Grace A. C. Bhaktivedanta Swami published the first Back to Godhead magazine in 1944. He also began to write translations and commentaries on Bhagavad-gita, Srimad-Bhagavatam, Caitanya-caritamrta, and other Vedic literatures. In 1965, after publishing three volumes of Srimad-Bhagavatam, he approached the owner of the Scindia Steam Navigation Company, Sumati Morarji, for a complimentary passage to the United States. After considering his request for some time, she finally agreed and issued him the ticket.

> In the port of Calcutta on August 13, 1965, carrying only a small suitcase, an umbrella, and a bag of dry cereal, A. C. Bhaktivedanta Swami, as he was known at the time, climbed up the steep gangway onto a cargo ship named the Jaladuta. The ensuing journey presented considerable hardship. Srila Prabhupada wrote of some sea-sickness, and on the thirteenth day of the voyage, during the passage through the Arabian Sea, he suffered a massive heart attack. He was concerned that he might pass away, but in his uneasy sleep that night he had a dream, a vision. Lord Krishna appeared. The Lord was in an open boat, along with His other incarnations. Krishna was rowing the boat, and the boat was pulling Srila Prabhupada's ship with a rope. Krishna was smiling at Srila Prabhupada and was pulling the ship all the way to America! Srila Prabhupada did not write about this occurrence in his diary but simply drew a line through those troubled days, declaring that he had passed

over a great crisis in the struggle between life and death. Years later he related these events to his followers.

After the crisis, Srila Prabhupada regained his strength and recommenced his entries in the diary after the ship docked in Port Said, Egypt. Then, after crossing the Mediterranean Sea, the Jaladuta passed through the Straits of Gibraltar and into the Atlantic Ocean. Uncharacteristically, the ocean appeared like a placid lake. The Atlantic crossing was so effortless that the ship's captain remarked that he had never seen anything like it. After a total of thirty-five days the ship at last berthed in Boston, at Commonwealth Pier, on September 17 at 5:30 a.m. The next day the Jaladuta continued to New York, where Srila Prabhupada disembarked onto a lonely Brooklyn pier to begin his mission in the West. *[Jaladuta Diary 1985]*

In this book (which is based on my realizations from 2001), I shall explain according to the evidence of the scriptures the true significance of this vision had by Srila Prabhupada. I also want to point out the spiritual benefits that can be obtained by gaining the correct understanding and subsequent worship of this transcendental pastime.

There is no difference in quality between Prahlad Maharaja seeing the Lord incarnate as Lord Nrsimhadeva and Srila Prabhupada seeing the Jaladuta incarnations. They are both transcendental pastimes to be worshiped and glorified by all devotees of the Lord. The manifestation of the Jaladuta incarnations is immensely significant, as they reveal the exalted position of Srila Prabhupada, his mission and the Lord's deep love for His dear devotee.

Our neglect to worship this transcendental pastime is due to our contaminated mentality of equating Prabhupada's loving dealings with the Lord to our own platform of duality in which dreams take place on the subtle material plane. For the pure devotee and the Lord there is no such material duality!

We have developed this offensive mentality of minimization and neglect due to our association, service and support of persons whose very existence is envy personified towards the pure devotee of the Lord Srila Prabhupada.

Prabhupada has exposed these demons as the envious dressed as devotees or the great sinister movement within his Krishna consciousness society. (See appendix 1 on page 106) He has clearly told us to completely neglect these jealous people in the dress of Vaisnavas:

A mundane person in the dress of a Vaisnava should not be respected but rejected. This is enjoined in the sastra (upeksa). The word upeksa means neglect. One should neglect an envious person. A preacher's duty is to love the Supreme Personality of Godhead, make friendships with Vaisnavas, show mercy to the innocent and reject or neglect those who are envious or jealous. **There are many jealous people in the dress of Vaisnavas in this Krishna consciousness movement, and they should be completely neglected**. There is no need to serve a jealous person who is in the dress of a Vaisnava. When Narottama dasa Thakura says chadiya vaisnava seva nistara payeche keba, he is indicating an actual Vaisnava, not an envious or jealous person in the dress of a Vaisnava. *[Caitanya Caritamrta Madhya Lila 1.218]*

Unfortunately, most devotees have completely neglected this important instruction. They have associated with and supported this envious movement of demons now controlling ISKCON and have thus neglected to worship Srila Prabhupada correctly as the most exalted devotee, who the Lord saved and carried safely across the Atlantic Ocean in his many forms.

Not only is this transcendental Jaladuta pastime not worshipped by devotees in ISKCON but it isn't even mentioned in the Vaishnava calendar. Yet in the same calendar we will find Yom Kippur, Hanukkah and Halloween. (See appendix 5 page 154) These are totally demoniac rituals that have no place in a calendar for devotees of Krishna. The fact that they are in the calendar proves clearly that the great sinister movement now controls ISKCON.

Yom Kippur can be summarised as follows: Be a Jew > Sin all Year > Transfer your sins to a chicken > Torture the chicken and kill it > The chicken goes to hell instead of you > Yay! We fooled God.

Hanukkah: The Jews celebration of their brutal supremacy over the non-jews or goyim (human animals).

Halloween: A celebration of Jewish ritual child sacrifice.

In the middle section of this book, I will explain the different versions of the Jaladuta and discuss the spiritual significance of the swastika which adorned it that was never seen by the devotee community.

Mukunda dasa   21/08/2022

CHAPTER ONE

Krishna Has Taken Charge Of The Ship

As you read through this book you will discover the sastric evidence which will prove beyond any doubt the factual position of Prabhupada and the Jaladuta Incarnations. Then this transcendental pastime will no longer be neglected but glorified by all the followers of Srila Prabhupada.

Our worship of this divine Jaladuta pastime will increase our knowledge and love for Srila Prabhupada and give us faith in the transcendental words he spoke on that momentous journey in 1965:

> Sri Srimad Bhaktisiddhanta Sarasvati Thakur, who is very dear to Lord Gauranga, the son of mother Saci, is unparalleled in his service to the Supreme Lord Sri Krishna. He is that great saintly spiritual master who bestows intense devotion to Krishna at different places throughout the world.
>
> By his strong desire, the holy name of Lord Gauranga will spread throughout all the countries of the Western world. In all the cities, towns and villages on the earth, from all the oceans, seas, rivers and streams, **everyone will chant the holy name of Krishna.**
>
> As the vast mercy of Sri Caitanya Mahaprabhu conquers all directions, a flood of transcendental ecstacy will certainly cover the land. When all the sinful, miserable living entities become happy, the Vaisnava's desire is then fulfilled. *[Prayer to the Lotus Feet of Krishna. Srila Prabhupada on board the Jaladuta steamship bound for America, September 13, 1965.]*

Now let us hear directly from the lotus mouth of the pure devotee Srila Prabhupada about his dream of the Lord, who appeared to him in His many forms.

The dream was that Krishna in His many forms was bowing the row

> Prabhupada: Hmm. The name is there, he remembered. After all, he is officer. He knows so many things. So it is a great history. (laughs) **There was two days I was attacked in heart on the ship. So hardship.**

Trivikrama: Then you had a dream?

Prabhupada: Hmm.

Hari-sauri: What was that, Srila Prabhupada?

Prabhupada: That is... (laughs) The dream was I must come here.

Hari-sauri: It was some instruction that you got?

Prabhupada: **The dream was that Krishna in His many forms was bowing the row. What is called?**

Hari-sauri: **Rowing the boat.**

Prabhupada: **Yes.**

[*Srila Prabhupada Room Conversation, June 8, 1976, Los Angeles*]

As we shall discover in the next chapter, Prabhupada's dreams are not like the dreams had by the conditioned souls, who are trapped in the grip of maya in this material world. The dreams of Srila Prabhupada are factual realized dealings with the Lord on the transcendental plane.

Lord Krishna has taken charge of the ship

Today I have disclosed my mind to my companion Lord Sri Krishna. There is a Bengali poem made by me today in this connection. At about eleven there is a little lurching. **The captain tells that they had never such calmness of the Atlantic. I said it is Lord Krishna's mercy.** His wife asked me to come back again with them so that they may have again a calm Atlantic Ocean. **If Atlantic would have shown its usual face perhaps I would have died. But Lord Krishna has taken charge of the ship**...... Today is the 33rd day of our journey and at 3 o'clock in the morning I saw the sky cloudy with dim moon-light. From morning till 1 o'clock the sky remained cloudy and at 1/30 p.m. there was a shower of rain. The sky is still cloudy and the wind is blowing from south-east corner and raining at intervals. The whole day passed in that way and the wind assumed a para-cyclonic face with dense cloud resulting in rain till 9/30 p.m. with regular lightening etc. At ten o'clock when I was talking in the captain's room the chief engineer Mr. Travers told me that he had never such experience of calm & quietness of the Atlantic Ocean. There was always typhoon, cyclone, fog, etc. at least for days in every trip in the past (?). **I said it is Lord Krishna's Grace. If such things as usual in Atlantic would have taken place, I would die.** *[Srila Prabhupada's Jaladuta Diary Monday 13th and Tuesday 14th September 1965]*

Prabhupada says that Lord Krishna had taken charge of the ship, calmed the sea and saved him from death due to the usual wild Altanic conditions. Again let us hear the words:

"Lord Krishna has taken charge of the ship"

This is very clear if we take Prabhupada's words with faith. Krishna in his many forms of incarnation was directly controlling the Jaladuta and the ocean. Prabhupada's journey on the Jaladuta was a wonderous transcendental pastime between the Lord and the pure devotee.

CHAPTER TWO

It Is All Factual; It Is Not A Dream

**The Lord, however, talks with the advanced
devotee, and the advanced devotee also sees
Him. It is all factual; it is not a dream.**

TRANSLATION " 'You know that I come and eat the offerings, but because of external separation, you consider this a dream.

PURPORT: Because mother Saci was feeling separation from Sri Caitanya Mahaprabhu, she thought she was dreaming that her son had come to her. Sri Caitanya Mahaprabhu, however, wanted to inform her that actually it was not a dream. He actually came there and ate whatever His mother offered Him. Such are the dealings of advanced devotees with the Supreme personality of Godhead. As stated in the Brahma-samhita:

premanjana-cchurita-bhakti-vilocanena
santah sadaiva hrdayesu vilokayanti
yam syamasundaram acintya-guna-svarupam
govindam adi-purusam tam aham bhajami

"I worship the primeval Lord, Govinda, who is always seen by the devotee whose eyes are anointed with the pulp of love. He is seen in His eternal form of Syamasundara, situated within the heart of the devotee." (Brahma-samhita 5.38) **pure devotees realize dealings with the Lord on the transcendental plane, but because the devotees are still in the material world, they think that these are dreams. The Lord, however, talks with the advanced devotee, and the advanced devotee also sees Him. It is all factual; it is not a dream.** [Srila Prabhupada from Caitanya Caritamrta Antya Lila 3.31]

Sri Caitanya Mahaprabhu, however, wanted to inform us that actually it was not a dream. He actually came there and rowed the boat in His many forms of incarnation. Such are the dealings of Srila Prabhupada with the Supreme Personality of Godhead. The Lord personally talked with Srila Prabhupada, and His Divine Grace also saw Him in His many forms rowing the Jaladuta to America. It was all factual; it was not a dream.

How exalted a devotee Srila Prabhupada must be that ALL THE INCARNATIONS MANIFEST to safely take him to the USA. I think we can understand from this transcendental pastime how important Srila Prabhupada's mission actually is. If anyone thinks that the demons can stop Prabhupada's preaching, they are completely deluded.

It cannot be checked. There may be so many hindrances. **But one who is pure devotee, his business cannot be stopped.** *[Prabhupada from a Srimad Bhagavatam Lecture 1.2.6. Calcutta. February 26th, 1974]*

Similarly, anyone who is ordered by the Lord to perform some action in this material world, especially preaching His glories, **cannot be counteracted by anyone**; the will of the Lord is executed under all circumstances. *[Srimad Bhagavatam 3.16.36]*

Similarly, since the sankirtana movement was first set in motion five hundred years ago by Sri Caitanya Mahaprabhu's desire that it spread all over the universe, the Krishna consciousness movement, in continuity of that same motion, is now spreading all over the world, and in this way **it will gradually spread all over the universe. With the spread of the Krishna consciousness movement, everyone will merge in an ocean of love of Krishna.** *[Caitanya Caritamrta Adi Lila 13.32]*

The Personality of Godhead manifests His multiforms according to the desires of the devotees... The Lord does not appear before the devotee because of the devotee's imagination

TRANSLATION: He approached the Personality of Godhead, who bestows all boons and who dispels the agony of His devotees and of those who take shelter of His lotus feet. He manifests His innumerable transcendental forms for the satisfaction of His devotees.

PURPORT: Here the words bhaktanam anurupatma-darsanam mean that **the Personality of Godhead manifests His multiforms according to the desires of the devotees.** For example, Hanumanji (Vajrangaji) wanted to see the form of the Lord as the Personality of Godhead Ramacandra, whereas other

Vaisnavas want to see the form of Radha-Krishna, and still other devotees want to see the Lord in the form of Laksmi-Narayana. The Mayavadi philosophers think that although all these forms are assumed by the Lord just as the devotees desire to see Him, actually He is impersonal. From Brahma-samhita, however, we can understand that this is not so, for the Lord has multiforms. It is said in the Brahma-samhita, advaitam acyutam. **The Lord does not appear before the devotee because of the devotee's imagination**. Brahma-samhita further explains that the Lord has innumerable forms: ramadi-murtisu kala-niyamena tisthan. He exists in millions and millions of forms. There are 8,400,000 species of living entities, but the incarnations of the Supreme Lord are innumerable. In the Bhagavatam it is stated that as the waves in the sea cannot be counted but appear and disappear continually, the incarnations and forms of the Lord are innumerable. *[Srila Prabhupada from Srimad Bhagavatam 3.20.25]*

The Lord did not appear before Srila Prabhupada because of Prabhupada's imagination. No, the Supreme Personality of Godhead directly appeared in His many forms of incarnation, saved His pure devotee and took direct charge of the Jaladuta rowing the boat to America. Thus the Lord fulfilled Prabhupada's desire to execute the order of Sri Srimad Bhaktisiddhanta Sarasvati Thakur.

The Lord can hear from such a distant place, and He can appear simultaneously in all places at a moment's notice. Such is the omnipotency of the Lord.

The Lord resides in His Vaikuntha planet. No one can estimate how far away this planet is situated. It is said, however, that anyone trying to reach that planet by airships or by mindships, traveling for millions of years, will find it still unknown. Modern scientists have invented airships which are material, and the yogis make a still finer material attempt to travel by mindships. The yogis can reach any distant place very quickly with the help of mindships. But neither the airship nor the mindship has access to the kingdom of God in the Vaikunthaloka, situated far beyond the material sky. Since this is the situation, how was it possible for the prayers of the elephant to be heard from such an unlimitedly distant place, and how could the Lord at once appear on the spot? These things cannot be calculated by human imagination. All this was possible by the unlimited power of the Lord, and therefore the Lord is described here as aprameya, for not even the best human brain can estimate His powers and potencies by mathematical calculation. **The Lord can hear from such a distant place, He can eat from there, and He can appear simultaneously in all places at a moment's notice. Such is the omnipotency of the Lord.** *[Srila Prabhupada from Srimad Bhagavatam 2.7.16]*

So the Lord after hearing the prayers of His pure devotee appeared at a moments notice in his multiforms before Srila Prabhupada. This cannot be calculated by human imagination. All this was possible by the unlimited power of the Lord and His love for His dear servant.

> **Similarly, no one can calculate when and how the different incarnations of the Lord appear according to the necessities of time, place and candidates.**

In the previous verses it has been described that although the Supreme Personality of Godhead has no material form, He accepts innumerable forms to favor His devotees and kill the demons. As stated in Srimad-Bhagavatam, there are so many incarnations of the Supreme Personality of Godhead that they are like the waves of a river. The waves of a river flow incessantly, and no one can count how many waves there are. **Similarly, no one can calculate when and how the different incarnations of the Lord appear according to the necessities of time, place and candidates.** *[Srila Prabhupada from Srimad Bhagavatam 8.3.12]*

So no one could have calculated that the Lord would appear in his many transcendental forms in the Arabian Sea. He did so to save Srila Prabhupada and safely rowed him to the United States of America.

Prabhupada has been especially chosen by the Lord to deliver Krishna consciousness to the whole world, lead an Aryan resurrection and thus liberate all the fallen souls.

> **There is no limit to the Lord's incarnations, but they can be perceived only by devotees who are fortunate.**

The incarnations of the Supreme Personality of Godhead appear continuously, like the waves of a river or an ocean. There is no limit to the Lord's incarnations, but they can be perceived only by devotees who are fortunate. *[Srila Prabhupada from Srimad Bhagavatam 10.2.42]*

**It is only by the personal sweet will of the Supreme
Personality of Godhead that He appears and
disappears, and only fortunate devotees can
expect to see Him face to face.**

All the incarnations described in the sastras act wonderfully
(kesava dhrta-mina-sarira jaya jagadisa hare). It is only by the
personal sweet will of the Supreme Personality of Godhead that
He appears and disappears, and only fortunate devotees can
expect to see Him face to face. *[Srila Prabhupada from Srimad
Bhagavatam 8.5.46]*

**Many Visnu incarnations expand at different ages
in the duration of the cosmic manifestation. They
are expanded only for the transcendental
happiness of the pure devotees**

From the Ksirodakasayi Visnu, many Visnu incarnations expand
at different ages in the duration of the cosmic manifestation.
They are expanded only for the transcendental happiness of the
pure devotees. The incarnations of Visnu, who appear at
different ages and times, are never to be compared to the
conditioned souls. The visnu-tattvas are not to be compared to
deities like Brahma and Siva, nor are they on the same level.
[Srila Prabhupada from Srimad Bhagavatam 3.9.2]

The Lord by His personal sweet will has appeared as the Jaladuta Incarnations
for the transcendental happiness of the most fortunate pure devotee Srila
Prabhupada. Now it is the time for us to worship this most amazing and
wonderful pastime and become blessed.

PRABHUPADA PROTECTED BY
THE JALADUTA INCARNATIONS

**When he was put into danger, then
Lord Nrsimhadeva came personally to give
him protection. That is the special duty of God.**

Just like Prahlada Maharaja. **When he was put into danger, then
Lord Nrsimhadeva came personally to give him protection.
That is the special duty of God. That is not unnatural.** If
somebody says, "God is partial, that He takes special care of His
devotee," no, that is not partiality. Just like a gentleman--in the

neighborhood, he loves all children, but when his own child is in danger, he takes special care. That is not unnatural. You cannot blame him that "Why you are taking special care of your own child?" No. That is natural. Nobody will blame him. Similarly, everyone is God's sons, **but His devotee is special. That is God's special attention. Ye tu bhajanti mam pritya tesu te mayi. So God is giving protection to every living entity, but if you become devotee of the Lord, pure devotee, without any motive, then God will take special care of you.** That is Krsna consciousness movement, that we are being harassed by maya, the material energy, and if we take shelter of Krsna then we will be specially protected. Mam eva prapadyante mayam etam taranti te.

[Prabhupada Lecture, Honolulu, May 25, 1975]

When Prabhupada was in a dangerous position aboard the Jaladuta, then Krishna in His many forms of incarnation came personally to give him protection. That is the special duty of God. Krishna gives special care and attention to his pure devotee Srila Prabhupada.

A devotee is always confident that "I am sincerely serving Krsna, so in case of danger Krsna will save me."

Prabhupada: Yes. **A devotee is always confident that "I am sincerely serving Krsna, so in case of danger Krsna will save me."** The, just like Prahlada Maharaja life we see. He was helpless child, and his father, great demon, always chastising him, but he was confident that Krsna would save him. So when the things became too much intolerable, so Lord appeared as Nrsimhadeva and killed Hiranyakasipu. **So therefore a devotee's protection by God is always guaranteed, and one who is pure devotee, he is not disturbed by any material condition. He keeps his firm faith in God. That is called surrender.** It is called avasya raksibe krsna visvasa palanam, to continue the faith that **"Krsna will give me protection."** This full suvrender means to accept things which is favorable to God consciousness, to reject things which is unfavorable to God consciousness, to have firm faith of security under the protection of God, to enter into the family of God. These are the different processes of surrender.

[Philosophy Discussions, William James]

Srila Prabhupada was always confident of Krishna's protection even when his death seemed certain. Prabhupada was not disturbed by the dangerous condition on the Jaladuta. He had firm faith in Krishna and thus his safety was guaranteed.

The Personality of Godhead who protects such pure devotees is known as the protector of the satvatas.

Bhagavan means the Almighty God who is the controller of all opulences, power, fame, beauty, knowledge and renunciation. He is the protector of His pure devotees. Although God is equally disposed to everyone, He is especially inclined to His devotees. Sat means the Absolute Truth. And persons who are servitors of the Absolute Truth are called satvatas. And **the Personality of Godhead who protects such pure devotees is known as the protector of the satvatas.**

[Prabhupada from Srimad Bhagavatam 1.1.12]

Understanding the influence of the Supreme Lord, he was surely fearless, since he understood that the Lord had appeared to give him protection

Struck with such great wonder, Vasudeva now concentrated his attention on the Supreme Personality of Godhead. **Understanding the influence of the Supreme Lord, he was surely fearless, since he understood that the Lord had appeared to give him protection** (gata-bhih prabhava-vit). Understanding that the Supreme Personality of Godhead was present, **he appropriately offered prayers as follows**.

[Prabhupada from Srimad Bhagavatam 10.3.12]

Struck with such great wonder, Srila Prabhupada now concentrated his attention on the Supreme Personality of Godhead. Understanding the influence of the Jaladuta incarnations, he was surely fearless, since he understood that the Lord had appeared to give him protection. Understanding that the Supreme

Personality of Godhead was present in His many forms of incarnation, he appropriately offered prayers as follows. (See chapter five - Prayers Written by Srila Prabhupada Aboard the Jaladuta - page 93)

CHAPTER THREE

The Spiritual Significance
Of The Jaladuta's Swastika

The following is taken from a video lecture I gave in 2018 and various articles I wrote thereafter.

If He Commits Some Mistake,
He Admits, "Yes." He Is Gentleman.

Prabhupada: Yes, actually. He must be standing on truth. That is greatness. Because "to err is human." Anyone commits mistake. There is no doubt about it. But after committing mistake, if I stick to that mistake, that is foolishness. When it is detected that it is mistake, you must admit. That is greatness.

[S.P.Morning Walk February 1, 1977, Bhubaneshwar]

Prabhupada: (chuckles) He is gentleman. He has admitted. A gentleman, if he commits some mistake, he admits, "Yes." He is gentleman. And if he persists on his mistake, he is rascal. He is a rascal. So he is a gentleman.

[S.P.Morning Walk July 18, 1975, San Francisco]

When I first put together my article and video about the three different versions of the Jaladuta I made a mistake. Only now as I have been compiling this book called Prabhupada and the Jaladuta Incarnations did Krishna reveal to me how my imperfect senses misinterpreted the pictures I was seeing.

My original article and video were called: PRABHUPADA NEVER TRAVELLED ON THE JALADUTA WE HAVE BEEN SHOWN!

Prabhupada Never Travelled On The Jaladuta We Have Been Shown!

Jaladuta 1

NO

Built - 1904
Purchased By
Scindia S.N. - 1922

Sold By
Scindia S.N. - 1926

Scrapped - ?

Jaladuta 2

NO

Built - 1927
Purchased By
Scindia S.N. - 1927

Sold By
Scindia S.N. - 1958

Scrapped - 1963

Jaladuta 3

YES

Built - 1959
Purchased By
Scindia S.N. - 1959

Scrapped - 1983

An Orwellian tactic to hide true history?

After discovering that there were three versions of the Jaladuta and finding different pictures of the ship, I put these pictures together in the collage shown above. At that time it seemed so clear to me, that the Jaladuta shown to us by ISKCON was not the ship that Prabhupada famously travelled on in 1965. The pictures I found were adorned with the swastika and looked bigger than that ship.

Only today by Krishna's grace did I see the error in my thinking. The Jaladuta shown to us by ISKCON was not a photograph of the front of the ship but it was taken from the rear. The angle of the picture makes the ship look smaller and the front of the ship it totally hidden from view. And because the back of the ship also has the word Jaladuta on it, it appears that it is the front of the ship moving from right to left. And because there is no swastika and the Jaladuta sign has also the words Bombay under it, the picture totally bewildered my intelligence. It appeared to be the smaller Jaladuta 2 and not the back of the Jaladuta 3.

Look clearly at the pictures and you will see the top of the funnel is angled in the opposite direction. The funnel is higher at the front and lower at the back. Other pictures I have now found clearly show the back view of the Jaladuta 3 with the Jaladuta Bombay markings.

So it is clear that I made a mistake in claiming Prabhupada didn't travel on the Jaladuta that ISKCON showed to everyone. Although my other points about the spiritual significance of the swastika on the ship that wasn't shown by ISKCON (either consciously or subconsciously) are still totally valid. Ultimately they were the main points of my presentation. In fact in one sense the mistake that I made has led to more people watching my video and reading my article and thus getting exposed to these main points. So my bewilderment was a blessing that helped to spread these real essential truths.

I wasn't the only one to make this mistake of taking the back of the Jaladuta 3 to be the front of another ship; namely Jaladuta 2. The proof of this can be found in the fact that even though I compiled my article many years ago, nobody to this day has refuted my false statement.

This is also confirmed by the following picture:

In this picture one can see the Jaladuta travelling backwards. The artist obviously thought like I did.

So why weren't we shown pictures of the front of the Jaladuta? It wasn't difficult to get photographs of this ship. Here are two pictures of the ship from 1960 and 1961:

The Jaladuta 3 was regularly travelling from India to Canada and America. So anybody could have visited ports in Vancouver or Boston and easily taken pictures of the ship. Or they could have requested pictures of it from the Scindia Steam Navigation Company.

If you go on google images and look for ships, the majority of the pictures will be of the front of the ship or a front/side view. A picture of the back/side view as with ISKCON's Jaladuta picture will not be the main picture to show a ship in its true beauty and glory.

Another point to consider; let us say you wanted to sell your car and needed to show pictures of it. Which of the following two pictures would you consider as your main picture?

Of course you would show the second picture. The front of the car is what gives the truest perspective of the car. It is the same with a picture of the Jaladuta. A rear view is incomplete and doesn't give the true look of the ship.

So why didn't any devotee try to get a picture with the correct frontal view of the Jaladuta? Well maybe the answer can be found in what is on the front of the ship; the swastika.

Take a look at another picture which clearly shows this:

Is this "mistake" of not presenting the front of the Jaladuta an Orwellian tactic to hide true history?

We shall discuss the possible motives behind this deceit later but let us now look at the websites in which I found these truths about the three Jaladuta ships.

There are actually three versions of the Jaladuta ship:

1. Jaladuta 1 was built in 1904. It was purchased by Scindia Steam Navigation Company in 1922 and was sold by them in 1926. The scrapped date for this ship is unknown at this time.
2. Jaladuta 2 which was built in 1927. It was purchased by Scindia in 1927 and sold by them in 1958. It was then scrapped in 1963.
3. Jaladuta 3 was built in 1959 and purchased by Scindia in 1959. It was later scrapped in 1983. This is the Jaladuta that Prabhupada travelled on to America.

The website called ShipsList was where I found some information. You can even see the weight of the three ships. Jaladuta 1 is 4,091 tonne, Jaladuta 2 is 4,996 and Jaladuta 3 is much larger at 9,177 tonnes. It also tells you the purchase dates etc.

I had to research, cross reference, different places to come up with my information, like in the following letter from Ted Finch. So this is the ShipsList Archive and there's some email correspondence from somebody called 'Das'. It seems like there was some devotee enquiring about this.

From: "Ted Finch" <mariners-l@efinch90.fsnet.co.uk>
Subject: Re: [TSL] info on Scindia S.N. Co. Ltd.--Jaladuta II
Date: Wed, 21 Feb 2007 21:14:15 -0000
References: <5.1.1.6.1.20070221153452.023b2c90@pop1.ns.sympatico.ca>

```
DAS,

It seems my previous reply didn't reach you!

JALADUTA 1927
4,966 gross tons, length 400ft x beam 52.0ft, speed 10 knots. Official
Number 153810. Built 1927 by Lithgows Ltd, Glasgow for Scindia S.N. Co,
Bombay.
1958 sold to Linea Adriatico Golfo Persa Ltda, Puerto Limon, Costa Rica
renamed AL DAMMAM
1958 resold same year to Cia Mar de Isola Spetsai, Puerto Limon (managed by
C. A. Petroutsis) renamed SPETSAI FORTUNE.
1961 renamed TRIESTE for same owner.
1963 scrapped at Split, Yugoslavia by Brodospas.
Information from Register of Merchant Ships built in 1927 by W. A. Schell.

Hope this is of assistance.

regards
Ted
----- Original Message -----
From: "Dusyant A. Sharma" <dusyant_108@yahoo.com>
To: <TheShipsList@rootsweb.com>
Sent: Wednesday, February 21, 2007 7:35 PM
Subject: [TSL] info on Scindia S.N. Co. Ltd.--Jaladuta II


>
> I am looking for info on the Jalduta II that was sold to the Linea
> Adriatico Gulfo Persa company in 1958 (possible) and was renmaed Al
> Dammam. The ship was previously operated by Scindia S.N. Co. Ltd.
> under the name Jaladuta. Regards.
>
> DAS
>
> University of Illinois at Chicago
> Chem.Engr. PhD candidate, May 2009
> ------------------------------------------
> visit TheShipsList Website
> http://www.theshipslist.com/
> ------------------------------------------
> To unsubscribe from the list, please send an email to
> THESHIPSLIST-request@rootsweb.com with the word 'unsubscribe' without the
> quotes in the subject and the body of the message
>
```

Here is another site I found:

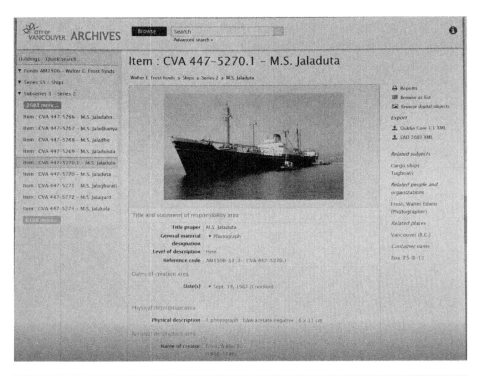

And on this site we see that the Jaladuta 3 was built in Germany:

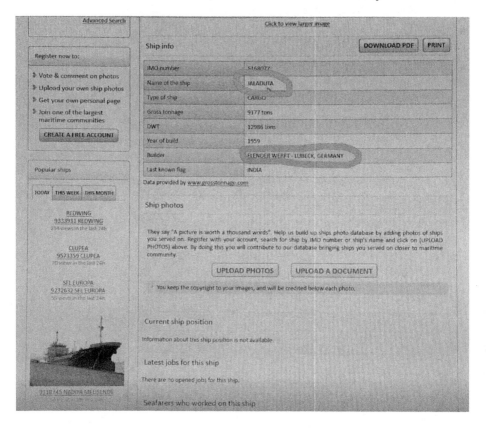

So the reason why the front of Jaladuta 3 wasn't shown to us was because it was adorned with a swastika. ISKCON is now completely controlled by Jews. As I said previously, it would not have been difficult for them to get pictures of the front of this ship. I really believe that these Jews controlling ISKCON (either consciously or subconsciously) did not want anyone to see the Jaladuta with its swastika on full view.

Jews actually hate the swastika and have had it banned in many countries after the Second World War and still try for banning it around the world even to this day, such is their revulsion of the sacred symbol.

On a deeper level we have to understand this aversion of the swastika by the Jews. You will discover as you read on in this chapter how the swastika is the symbol of a Godly fight against demonism.

Prabhupada's ship adorned with its beautiful swastika has such deep meaning in the continuation of this fight for Mother Earth. It represents the rise of Aryan consciousness and the ultimate defeat of demonism.

With this in mind it makes perfect sense why the deviant Jews controlling and destroying ISKCON would not resonate with this symbol. Why would there be an intense desire and search by the corrupt leaders of ISKCON to find a proper picture of the Jaladuta with its glorious front side on full view?

That picture with the deep spiritual meaning that it carries was far too heavy to bear in a time of ignorance created by the rogues and non-devotees working for the side of demonism.

The picture of the Jaladuta with its swastika had to be revealed at a later time, when truth was stronger and the lies were fleeing like a mist at sunrise.

Therefore I say the Jewish leaders of ISKCON didn't even want to obtain that picture, what to speak of revealing it to the world thus linking the fight of Adolf Hitler to the Messiah foretold by him, in the subconscious mind of humanity.

Now let us look more deeply into the significance of all this.

As discussed earlier, the Jaladuta 3 was built in Germany. This is also another clear sign. It is carrying the swastika. But people will say that this is just the Indian swastika and it has no connection to the Nazi flag. The real question to ask then is this: Why did Hitler mark his flag with a swastika?

The answer is given very clearly by Srila Prabhupada in the following quote. (Note: This quote was suppressed by the Jewish leaders of ISKCON for over 40 years; it was discovered recently by a friend of mine – If they have hidden this quote and the truth that Prabhupada spoke in regards Hitler never killing 6 million Jews, then hiding or not getting a front facing picture of the Jaladuta is nothing for them.)

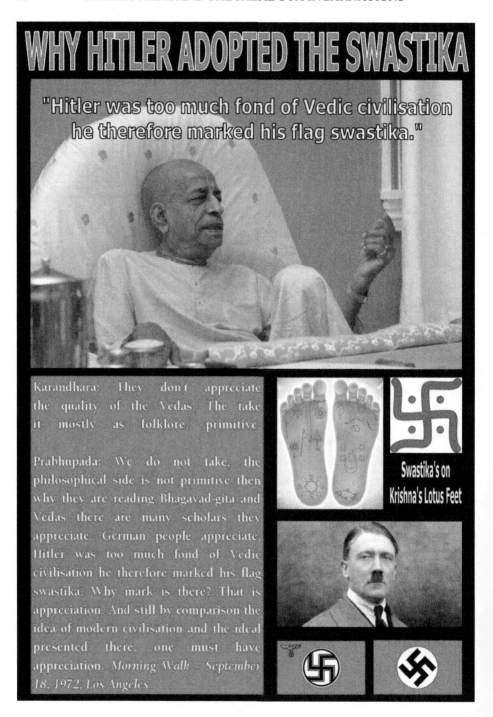

Karandhara: They don't appreciate the quality of the Vedas. The take it mostly as folklore, primitive.

Prabhupada: We do not take, the philosophical side is not primitive then why they are reading Bhagavad-gita and Vedas there are many scholars they appreciate. **German people appreciate. Hitler was too much fond of Vedic civilization he therefore marked his flag swastika. Why mark is there? That is appreciation.** And still by comparison the idea of modern civilization and the ideal presented there, one must have appreciation. *[Srila Prabhupada Morning Walk — September 18, 1972, Los Angeles]*

So the answer is very clear. Hitler was too much fond of Vedic civilization and therefore he marked his flag with the swastika. We should also understand that Vedic civilization is non-different than Krishna himself as he is the creator of the civilization.

According to the three modes of material nature and the work ascribed to them, the four divisions of human society were created by Me. **And, although I am the creator of this system**, you should know that I am yet the non-doer, being unchangeable. *[Bhagavad-gita 4.34]*

Therefore the statement could also be understood as follows:

Hitler was too much fond of Krishna so therefore he marked his flag with the swastika.

To be fond of Vedic civilization is to be fond of the culture of the Supreme Lord Sri Krishna. This is tantamount to being too much fond (affectionate) of Krishna.

This would be further supported by the fact that Hitler was a great student of the Bhagavad-gita (The words spoken by Lord Krishna).

Hitler was a great student of Bhagavad-gita.

Hitler was a great student of Bhagavad-gita. And there were many scholars still reading Bhagavad-gita, trying to understand. Just see what best depth of knowledge He has given. It is made by Kṛṣṇa. So in knowledge, in wealth, in strength, in beauty, and in everything He was opulent. Therefore He is Bhagavan. You cannot accept any ordinary man as Bhagavan. *[Prabhupada from a Bhagavad-gita Lecture 2.7-11, New York, March 2, 1966]*

I received the following email message from Hamsaduta dasa prabhu:

"Because Prabhupada knew I was born in Germany (Berlin, May 27 1941) and could speak German, he sometimes mentioned some small facts in moments of confidential association regarding Adolf Hitler. Usually when i was the secretary, when we were alone in his room, or travelling somewhere in his car. **He once mentioned that Hitler's abend buch (evening book), the book one keeps on a small bedside desk that he reads shortly before taking rest, was BHAGAVAD Gita.**"

Now let us look in more detail in regards to the reasoning for marking the flag with a certain symbol. The following quote from Prabhupada is very revealing:

Kapi-dhvajah. Kapi-dhvajah is also significant. Kapi-dhvajah, Arjuna, on his... Just like nowadays also, every nation has different types of flags, so Arjuna also had his flag on the... Dhvajah. Dhvajah means the flag. The flag was on the top of his chariot. And it was marked with Hanuman, Vajrangaji, Vajrangaji, Hanuman, who fought for Lord Ramacandra. He is fighting for Krishna. So he is also following the footsteps of Vajrangaji. Vaisnavism is like that. Mahajano yena gatah sa panthah. Mahajano yena gatah sa panthah. Vaisnava should follow his previous mahajana, authority. That is Vaisnavism. We don't manufacture ideas. We don't commit such rascaldom. We simply accept the behavior or the activities of previous acaryas. There is no difficulty. There is no difficulty. So in the fighting principle, **Arjuna is fighting for Krishna. He is following the previous fighting acarya, Hanumanji.**

Therefore he has depicted his flag with Hanuman, that "Hanumanji, Vajrangaji, kindly help me." This is Vaisnavism. "I have come here to fight for Lord Krishna. You fought also for the Lord. Kindly help me." This is the idea. Kapi-dhvajah. So any activities of the Vaisnava, they should always pray to the previous acarya, "Kindly help me. Kindly…" This is, Vaisnava is always thinking himself helpless, helpless. And begging help from the previous acarya. *[Prabhupada Lecture Bhagavad-gita 1.20, London, July 17, 1973]*

The marking of a flag has great significance. Arjuna in great humility was seeking the blessing of the previous fighting acarya Hanumanji, so he could gain victory in the battle of Kuruksetra. In the same way we can understand that Hitler sought Krishna's blessing with the swastika so he could gain victory and defeat atheistic Jewish communism.

There is always a fight for Mother Earth between the demons and the devotees, there is always this battle going on.

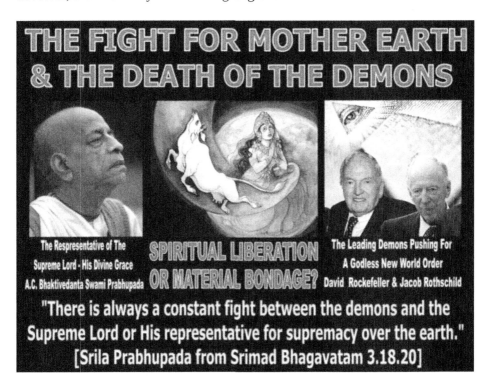

The fight between the Lord, the Supreme Personality of Godhead, and the demon is compared to a fight between bulls for the sake of a cow. The earth planet is also called go, or cow.

As bulls fight between themselves to ascertain who will have union with a cow, **there is always a constant fight between the demons and the Supreme Lord or His representative for supremacy over the earth**. *[Srila Prabhupada from Srimad Bhagavatam 3.18.20]*

After Krishna departed from this earth over 5,000 years ago, the world has gradually become more and more under the control of the demons. Their goal is to get total domination of the earth and its resources and rule over all the people with Godless tyranny.

In the last one hundred or more years they have mainly used communism as their vehicle to achieve this goal. We should understand very clearly that the communism movement was created, funded and totally controlled from the top by international Jewry (See appendix 3 on page 137)

Communism is totally Jewish, and that demoniac regime was behind the Bolshevik revolution that took over Russia through an internal revolution and went on to kill 60 million Russian people.

That same demoniac revolution was growing all over Europe but was checked by Adolf Hitler, who prevented it from spreading by standing up against international Jewry.

So even though Hitler may have externally lost the Second World War because he couldn't fully protect Germany and build what he had envisioned for Europe, on a deeper level he was victorious. Hitler was empowered by the Lord to protect the west. He stopped or slowed down the spread of communism in Europe, just long enough to allow for Srila Prabhupada to come and deliver the final solution in the rest of the free world.

Hitler was used as an agent of the Lord to preserve a field, namely Christian Europe, because Europe and America were built on the moral values of Christianity. Jesus Christ is a pure devotee exactly like Prabhupada. He descended to deliver the message of how to go back to Godhead, in a particular time, place and circumstance. So that message that he gave was still, on some small level, still existing in western civilization. Had Hitler not stopped the march of communism (the march of international Jewry), then that demoniac tyranny would have been like a tsunami and it would have completely overwhelmed Europe and America, to such a degree that there would no longer be any freedom. 1984 in one sense was probably the target date for the demons to have the whole world lockdown under tyrannical communism. So Hitler was victorious because he protected Europe from total communist control.

Hitler himself actually knew he was doing the preparatory work for the man to come.

> I know that some Man capable of giving our problems a final solution must appear. I have sought such a man. I could nowhere discover him. And that is why I have set myself to do the preparatory work (die Vorarbeit); only the most urgent preparatory work, for I know that I am myself not, the one. And I know also what is missing in me (to be the one). But the other One still remains aloof, and nobody comes forward, and there is no moretime to be lost. *[Adolf Hitler to Hans Grimm in 1928]*

The wonderful preparatory work that Adolf Hitler did for the Lord was to check the spread of Jewish controlled atheistic communism just enough to allow Prabhupada to come and deliver the final solution to the problem of that demoniac civilization. The world owes a great debt to that brave and wonderful warrior Adolf Hitler. The Lord empowered him and all the courageous pious souls of Europe to fight against all the odds the most powerful demoniac forces on earth. Their brave struggle slowed the demons march for world domination down just enough to allow for the appearance of that divine soul that was so eagerly sought after by Hitler. What is actually taking place in this world right now is the eternal struggle or spiritual warfare between the forces of divine and demoniac. And contrary to what the demons have been telling us for the last 70 to 80 years, Hitler's fight was supremely divine. Now is the time that we all play our part in this great fight and cleanse the demons from within ourselves by taking shelter of that one who is no longer aloof. This is where our battle begins!

> Thank you Lord Krishna, for sending and empowering Adolf Hitler to protect our western Christian civilizations, from the barbaric terror of the Jewish Bolsheviks.

> O Lord, let us always remain deeply grateful and never forget that the freedoms we still now retain in our nations, are due to the brave fight and ultimate sacrifice made by Hitler and the Waffen SS.

Their righteous struggle against evil has surely allowed you to send your Divine messenger Srila Prabhupada to our still fertile soils.

For had they not checked this demoniac Bolshevik terror, then our lands would have been totally barren of God consciousness, full of tyranny and slavery.

The Jewish Bolsheviks are now waging war on the moral foundations of our civilizations, through their cultural marxist revolution.

O Lord, Srila Prabhupada has been sent by You to deliver to our hearts your holy names and thus counteract this demoniac plan to destroy humanity.

Let us not misuse our freedom which so many have sacrificed and died to preserve. Let us not be drowned and carried away by moral decay.

Jesus said "Our Father, who art in heaven hallowed be thy name; thy kingdom come, thy will be done, on earth as it is in heaven."

O Lord, let us all take your hallowed names: Hare Krishna, Hare Krishna, Krishna Krishna, Hare Hare. Hare Rama, Hare Rama, Rama Rama, Hare Hare. And again revive our Aryan culture.

For it is only through the power of Aryan purity that we can defeat the eternal enemies of mankind.

 "Glorify the name of your Lord, the most high." Koran 87.2

"Everyone who calls upon the name of the Lord will be saved" Saint Paul, Romans10.13

"All who sincerely call upon my name will come to me after death and I will take them to paradise." Vows of Buddha 18

"From the rising of the sun to its setting, the name of the Lord is to be praised." King David, Psalms 113.3

Prayer by Mukunda dasa.

Hitler spoke again about the man to come calling him a Messiah who will start a new religion that will change the world.

'Do you believe in God?' I asked, gazing at him directly. Hitler looked at me in surprise, then smiled and said: 'Yes – I believe in a divine power, not in the dogmas of the Church, although I consider them necessary. I believe in God and in a divine destiny.' He turned away then and, folding his hands, gazed into the distance. **'And when the time is ripe, a new Messiah will come – he doesn't have to be a Christian, but he will found a new religion that will change the world.'** *[Leni Riefenstahl (Memoirs, p.g. 211)]*

He also said that we should all fight for this Messiah.

In the Bunker, shortly before his disappearance, an SS officer asked Hitler:

"Mein Fuhrer, for whom shall we fight now?"

Hitler responded: "For the man who will come." *[Miguel Serrano – Adolf Hitler The Ultimate Avatar]*

That Messiah is Srila Prabhupada who came on the Jaladuta adorned with the swastika carried by all the incarnations of the Lord.

On the subtle plane of existence the demons are already defeated. Over 500 years Lord Caitanya delared:

Prithvite ache yata nagaradi grama
sarvatra prachara haibe mora nama

In as many towns and villages as there are on the surface of the earth, My holy name will be preached. *[Chaitanya Bhagavata]*

These words have caused their destruction. The will of the Lord is executed under all circumstances. Now the Lord has sent his divine messenger Srila Prabhupada to complete the task.

Now the demons are just hanging on for dear life, the knockout punch has been delivered; the demons are just reeling about in the ring almost ready to drop to the floor in total defeat. They are finished!!!

Prabhupada has delivered this spiritual revolution with the full backing and power of the Jaladuta Incarnations, who could stop it?

This revolution will spiritualise the world. The foundations have been laid, the spiritual books are there and these books will be the law books for mankind for the next 10,000 years. Everyone will take shelter of Srila Prabhupada and by his guidance they will all be able to become free of material contamination and become pure themselves, fit for returning back to Godhead.

So the whole world is going to be organised in such a way that the souls on the planet can fulfil their birth right, which is to become fully purified and go back to God. That is our birth right. When we take birth as a human being, we have the great boon of the human life and we have the facility to go back to Godhead, if we get shelter of the pure devotee. So Srila Prabhupada lives in sound, he lives in his teachings, he lives in his books.

> **So we should associate by the vibration, and not by the physical presence. That is real association. Sabdad anavrtti. By sound.** Just like we are touching Krishna immediately by sound. Sound vibration. **So we should give more stress on the sound vibration, either of Krishna or of the spiritual master. Then we'll feel happy and no separation.** *[S.P. Lecture, 18/8/68, Montreal]*

> So although a physical body is not present, **the vibration should be accepted as the presence of the spiritual master, vibration. What we have heard from the spiritual master, that is living.** *[S.P. Lecture, 13/1/69, Los Angeles.]*

My Guru Maharaja used to say, **"Don't try to see a saintly person by your eyes. You see a saintly person by the ear."** Because if you hear from the saintly person and if he is speaking from the experience which he has heard from the, another saintly person--this is called guru-parampara--then the knowledge is perfect. *[S.B. Lecture 6.1.42, Los Angeles 8th June 1976.]*

Adolf Hitler was empowered by the Lord and he had great spiritual awareness so he adopted the swastika. I think that is very significant. It is like Hitler is showing that he is part of the plan. He played his part. People may say "if Krishna wanted Prabhupada to come and deliver this message, he would of done it regardless of what Hitler did." But that is a foolish statement. The fact of the matter is that Adolf Hitler did check the spread of demoniac communism, atheistic Jewish communism and he stopped it. He checked it, he didn't stop it completely but he checked it just enough so that the whole western civilization would not be completely lost. There was still some fertile ground, moral ground, some civilization instead of life becoming totally demoniac and barbaric. So in this way there was still something, some glimmer of civilization left, something left for Prabhupada to come to.

When Prabhupada went to America he never got checked. When he went to Russia he was getting harassed. He couldn't go to Russia and sit there in a park and chant Hare Krishna and spread Krishna consciousness. No, that was not possible in communist Russia.

So if Adolf Hitler wouldn't have fought the Jewish communists, then whatever came to pass in Russia (such as people been taken away to Gulags, being killed, with no freedoms at all), that was coming for the rest of Europe. Do your research on this, look at what the Jews did to the Russians, who were mainly Christians, they were not atheists, they were not communists, but Christians.

The Bolshevik revolution in Russia wasn't a revolution from within the country by the dissatisfied workers. It was actually a revolution from without. The Jewish leaders, mainly came from America funded by big bankers like Jacob Schiff. So from without they came in and took over. They created a civil war with the Russia people and then took control of the country and killed millions of people.

So whatever went on in Russia, if it wasn't for Adolf Hitler being empowered, it was coming to the rest of Europe and the world. Just look at what Adolf Hitler did. No ordinary human could have done what he did in Germany unless he was empowered. He was the closest thing we see to a Vedic leader in this Kali Yuga or the age of quarrel.

There are four ages in the universe that go in a cycle, like spring, summer, autumn and winter. So Kali yuga is like the winter, we are now in the winter of this universal cycle, there is not much religion left. But Adolf Hitler by the way he looked after his people is the closest thing we can see to a real Vedic King.

So whatever happened in Russia would have happened in Germany. That is what the communists were trying to do in Germany, they were trying for that revolution. But Hitler checked that internal attack, so they attacked him from without. They failed to bring Germany down from within. So they attacked from without, nearly the whole world attacked, that is the Second World War. And Hitler put up an amazing fight because the Lord empowered him to check them.

Therefore the Jews with their communism could only go half way through Germany. The Berlin wall marked the end of their tyrannical border. In one sense the Berlin wall was very symbolic as communism stopped there in its gross form. And from the Berlin wall going west it kept some freedoms; it maintained some remnants of the Christian civilization it was built on.

It was also still fertile enough for Prabhupada to come there and preach. Just like when Prabhupada freely came to America in 1965, he was so pleased to see so many churches. So Prabhupada came to continue the mission of Jesus Christ and revive Krishna consciousness, spiritual consciousness. And he did that in America and Europe because Adolf Hitler preserved those countries by his great fight against communism. This is the clear fact.

So let us not disregard Hitler. He was the Lord's instrument. When the Lord uses someone then that person is an instrument of the Lord. So one may say that the Lord can use anyone or if Krishna wanted Prabhupada to preach then Krishna could have done anything. But the fact is the Lord used Hitler. This is the FACT. So there is no point saying ifs and buts. Today I just posted a crude example on Facebook that nicely illustrates my point. I said "If my Grandma had a pair of testicles she would be my Grandad. But my Grandma doesn't have a pair of testicles so she is my Grandma and my Grandad does have a pair of testicles so he is my Grandad." So Adolf Hitler, HE DID IT, nobody else did it. Respect it. It is as simple as that.

So it is very significant that the Jaladuta 3 had the the swastika on the front. To me it is so significant. Prabhupada could have come on any ship. He could have got a free ticket with another Indian steam shipping company but he got a free ticket to go on the Jaladuta. He didn't get a free ticket to go on another ship, with another company that didn't have the swastika on the front. Not all Indian shipping companies carry the swastika on their ships.

And the ship was called the Jaladuta. Jala meaning water or ocean and duta means messenger. So the messenger over the ocean, on a ship adorned with the swastika. "Oh… it's just a coincidence." NO!!! Everything is under the control of the Lord, especially the actions of a pure devotee. So Prabhupada came on the Jaladuta with the swastika, to show that he was coming to finish the work that Hitler had done in fighting demonism. Prabhupada wasn't just coming to fight it, but to finish it. To end it for good by bringing in the spiritual revolution that shall deliver the whole human civilization.

PRABHUPADA'S "CONTRADICTORY" STATEMENTS ABOUT HITLER RESOLVED

Prabhupada's statements about Hitler being a demon are as true as his statements about the Sun being 93 million miles from Earth. They are "truths" spoken at a particular time, place and circumstance.

The few statements Prabhupada made about Hitler being a demon were largely spoken to an audience that had fully accepted the lies they were told by the Jewish bankers after the end of the Second World War. The real truth Prabhupada spoke of Hitler was totally different. In this article i hope to clear these apparent contradictions.

You say that there is some contradiction in Prabhupada's statements about Hitler, that is your defective understanding because you are not advanced in knowledge.

You say that there is some contradiction in the Bhagavad-gita, that is your defective understanding. The direct meaning of the 15th Chapter 7th verse is that every living entity is the eternal part and parcel of Krishna. How can you think of contradiction in the Bhagavad-gita? Krishna is not an ordinary human being. How can you think that Krishna is contradicting Himself in His own statements? It is your concoction. The jiva is jivatma and Krishna is paramatma. Where is the contradiction? Why do you manufacture "iva"? That is the defect of Mayavadi philosophy. They concoct ideas. *[Srila Prabhupada Letter to: Sri K. Raghupati Rao, Calcutta 13 January, 1976]*

Therefore it is said, śrutayo vibhinnā. There are innumerable Vedic scriptures. So we cannot come to the conclusion what is right or wrong, **because sometimes you will find contradiction from one... Of course, there is no contradiction, but because we are not advanced in knowledge, sometimes we will find contradiction.** Just like in India there are two classes of transcendentalists: the impersonalist and the personalist. That is not contradiction. The Absolute Truth is both impersonal and personal, but somebody is stressing on the impersonal point of view and somebody is stressing on the personal point of view. *[Prabhupada Pandal Lecture, Delhi, November 20, 1971]*

There can be no contradiction in the statements of Prabhupada about Hitler. Our lack of knowledge may make it appear that there is, but actually there are NO CONTRADICTIONS! This is the basis of the rest of my article.

Prabhupada said many many times that the Sun was 93 million miles away from the Earth. Does that actually mean it really is?

So although the Supreme Lord is far, far away... Of course, He is not far, far away, but in our conception, in the material conception, because we cannot see... We are on a different planet. So by His energy He is not far away. Just like the sunlight, the sunshine, in the morning you find the sunshine is within your room, the sun is just within your room. It is actually. **But still, the sun is 93,000,000 miles away from you.** Similarly, in all circumstances we must understand that Krishna is, although far away from us, still, He is with us, within us. This is called knowledge. This is called knowledge. *[Prabhupada from a Bhagavad-gita 4.20-24 New York, August 9, 1966]*

Krishna says that "I am expanded in My impersonal feature everywhere. But I am not there." It is very simple to understand. Just like the sunshine. The sunshine is expanded all over the universe. But if you are in the sunshine, you cannot say that "I am in the sun planet." No, that is not. **Sun planet is**

93,000,000's miles away. But the sunshine is not different from the sun. That is also fact. But still, you cannot say, because the sunshine has entered in your room, you cannot say that "I am in direct connection with the sun-god or the sun planet." No. This is called acintya-bhedabheda philosophy: "simultaneously, inconceivably, one and different." So everything is God. That is a fact. And still, everything is not God. That is also fact. So we have to understand this philosophy.   *[Prabhupada from a Srimad-Bhagavatam 1.2.6, Delhi, November 12, 1973]*

They are going to, trying to go to the moon planet but according to our calculation they have never gone to the moon planet. They have never gone because, we find in the sastras, the moon planet is situated 1,600,000 miles above the sun. **And they calculate that 93,000,000's of miles the sun is situated. So 93,000,000 plus another 1,600,000 it becomes 95,000,000 miles.** How one can go ninety-five millions of miles in four days? So according to our sastra, we cannot believe this statement. *[Prabhupada from a Bhagavad-gita 3.27, Madras, January 1, 1976]*

So here we see a few examples of Prabhupada saying that the sun is 93 million miles from Earth. These are "truths" spoken according to audiences who had generally accepted the materialistic scientists vision of the universe. Prabhupada spoke these circumstantial "truths" about the Sun's position to support a particular point he was making.

Yet when asked directly about the position of the Sun in relation to the Earth, Prabhupada spoke FACTUAL TRUTH and not the "truth" according to time place and circumstance.

Prabhupada: (in car) They have not gone to the moon planet.
Paramahamsa: Really?
Prabhupada: Yes. It is far, far away. Their calculation is wrong. They are going to a wrong planet.
Paramahamsa: It must be the Rahu planet.
Prabhupada: Yes, or something else. Not moon planet.
Paramahamsa: How many...
Prabhupada: It is above the sun planet.
Paramahamsa: Moon planet is further?

Prabhupada: Yes.

Paramahamsa: Oh. Because they say that the moon planet is the closest planet to the earth. That is their calculation. And they say that it orbits around the earth, and then that the earth orbits the sun.

Prabhupada: **All wrong**. What is the... According to them, what is the distance of sun planet?

Paramahamsa: **Sun planet is 93,000,000 miles.**

Ganesa: They say the moon planet is only 250,000 miles.

Prabhupada: **It is wrong thing.**

Paramahamsa: **Is their calculation for the distance of the sun wrong also?**

Prabhupada: **Yes.**

[Srila Prabhupada Morning Walk, May 12, 1975, Perth]

If one studies the Fifth Canto chapter twenty two of Srimad Bhagavatam one will find the actual distance of the Sun above the earth as 800,000 miles!

Prabhupada spoke of Hitler as a good man, a gentleman. This is the factual truth!

So just as Prabhupada spoke a circumstantial "truth" about the Sun, he spoke the same circumstantial "truths" about Hitler as follows:

> We have seen. There were so many asuras [demons] in this world. There were Lenin, there were Stalin, there were Hitler, there were Hiraṇyakaśipu. So many. But they could not survive. It is not possible. They'll be finished.
>
> *[Prabhupada from a Srimad-Bhagavatam 1.8.20, Mayapura, September 30, 1974]*

After the Second World War, due to the vigorous propaganda of the Jewish bankers the whole world was led to believe that Hitler was the greatest demon that ever lived or the devil incarnate. This was the deep seated consciousness of the large majority of the people in the world.

It was to these very people that Prabhupada was introducing the science of Krishna Consciousness and therefore **he spoke to them the circumstantial "truth" that their ears could bear to hear.**

The FACTUAL TRUTH of Hitler was spoken by Prabhupada as follows:

**He was a good man... therefore I don't believe that
he killed so many Jews in concentration camps.**

Paramahamsa: Adolf Hitler was vegetarian.
Prabhupada: Eh?
Paramahamsa: Adolf Hitler was vegetarian.
Prabhupada: Who?
Paramahamsa: Adolf Hitler.
Svarupa Damodara: Hitler.
Prabhupada: **Ah. He was a good man.**
Paramahamsa: Oh!
Prabhupada: **Therefore he did not drop the atomic bomb.**
Paramahamsa: Yes I agree.
Prabhupada: Your Truman dropped.
Paramahamsa: Not my Truman.
Prabhupada: Yes your Truman your president. Paramahamsa:
I'm not American.
Devotees: [laughter]
Prabhupada: **He hesitated; therefore I don't believe that he
killed so many Jews in concentration camps.** Paramahamsa:
But actually Hitler he was trying to invent the atom bomb, but
the Americans invented it before before Tru.. The Americans
invented it before the Nazis did.
Prabhupada: No no the Americans stolen..
Svarüpa Damodara: The German Germans invented the atomic..
The Germans first..
Paramahamsa: [indistinct] they had the plan but they could not
invent it.
Prabhupada: No what they drop dropped in Japan that was
German.. technology arrangement…

[Prabhupada Morning Walk -- October 8, 1972, Berkeley]

This quote was hidden by the Jewish leaders of ISKCON for over 45 years! It
was recently discovered by one nice devotee doing transcribing work for
Bhaktivedanta archives.

So he's advertised very adversely, but if it is a true fact, then how he could have this human consideration that he did not throw the nuclear weapon?

So far, of course, I know that this nuclear weapon was already discovered by the German people and Hitler, it is said that he did not use it. Because he knew it that "If I throw this nuclear weapon there will be devastation." **So from this point it can be considered that he had some human consideration. So he's advertised very adversely, but if it is a true fact, then how he could have this human consideration that he did not throw the nuclear weapon?** And this was taken by the Americans and it was thrown in Japan. That is the history so far we know. *[Prabhupada from a Śrīmad-Bhāgavatam Lecture 1.7.19 Vrndavana, September 16, 1976]*

He was gentleman. But these people are not gentlemen. He knew it perfectly well. He said that "I can smash the whole world, but I do not use that weapon."

Dr. Patel: Yes, sir, but it is said that the German scientist ran away to America because they were afraid of Hitler. If Hitler gets the secret of atom, he would bomb out the whole world.
Prabhupāda: No, no. Hitler knew it.
Dr. Patel: No. They were not able to be successful to...
Prabhupāda: No, no. He knew it, everything, but he did not like to do it. He said. He said. **He was gentleman. But these people are not gentlemen. He knew it perfectly well. He said that "I can smash the whole world, but I do not use that weapon." The Germans already discovered. But out of humanity they did not use it.** And all the, your American, other countries, they have stolen from German ideas. *[Prabhupada Morning Walk, November 20, 1975, Bombay]*

So Prabhupada is saying that Hitler was a gentleman but these people are not gentlemen. Who are these people??? They are the atheist communist Jewish bankers who are the real demoniac tyrants of the world!!

So these English people, they were very expert in making propaganda. They killed Hitler by propaganda. I don't think Hitler was so bad man.

Prabhupada: Ah, yes. **So these English people, they were very expert in making propaganda. They killed Hitler by propaganda. I don't think Hitler was so bad man**. What do you think? You are Englishman. (laughter)

Hari-sauri: It's getting.... (laughs) Just from hearing you speak in the last few months **I can understand that the whole history that I was ever presented in school is completely warped around to the way that the English saw it**, especially the last two centuries, when the British empire was on the move. It's completely... *[Prabhupada Room Conversation, June 17, 1976, Toronto]*

Hitler fought very valiantly and thus displayed the qualities of a ksatriya warrior

Just like in Europe, that Hitler, he wanted supremacy over Europe, and **he fought very valiantly**. But at the end he became vanquished. Similarly, in the material world we have got so many desires and we want to fulfill it—and for which we work very hard. But at the end it becomes frustrated. That is the nature of the material world. *[Prabhupada Lecture, London, September 14, 1969]*

Here we see Prabhupada describe Hitler as fighting very valiantly. Let's look at the dictionary definition of the word valiant:

Full Definition of valiant:

1. possessing or acting with **bravery** or boldness : **courageous** <valiant soldiers>

2. marked by, exhibiting, or carried out with **courage or determination** : **heroic** <valiant feats>

Sounds just like the Lord's description of a ksatriya [pious fighting warrior] in the Bhagavad-gita.

> Heroism, power, determination, resourcefulness, courage in battle, generosity, and leadership are the qualities of work for the kṣatriyas. *[Bhagavad-gita As It Is (1972) 18.43]*

Prabhupada said Hitler fought very valiantly but was vanquished. Still we should also understand that his brave fight against the Jewish bankers and their demoniac red terror of communism has helped the sankirtana movement.

Had Hitler not fought the bankers so bravely, then the world would have been a different place and Prabhupada wouldn't have been able to come and preach Krishna Consciousness, just as he wasn't allowed to Preach in Russia. The world would have been totally under the control of atheistic communism.

If Prabhupada's movement had more devotees like Sulocana dasa prabhu, who had a brave heart like Hitler and actually fought against the Jewish agents in the Krishna Consciousness movement instead of surrendering blindly and ever so obediently to them, then perhaps we might now have a powerful Krishna Consciousness preaching movement with self-sufficient farm communities that could give real shelter to the suffering people of the world!

"Hitler Lovers, Jew Haters"
The mirror projections of the bewildered
who don't want to face FACTUAL TRUTH.

There are people who are very angry to hear the factual truth of Hitler and the lies of the Jewish holocaust. Thus in their denial they project in mirror form their own hatred on to the truth givers. "You are Hilter lovers and Jew haters and are twisting Prabhupada's words and making him look the same."

Actually they are Hitler haters, holocaust supporters and Jewish sympathizers. Or how else can they not accept the FACTUAL TRUTH THAT PRABHUPADA SPEAKS!!!

THE TIMES THEY ARE A CHANGING
"Speaking the truth will give a bad name to the
Jewish controlled Krishna Conscious Movement"

There are others, who although accepting the factual truth that Prabhupada spoke about Hitler, say that such truths should remain hidden and that they will only bring a bad name to Prabhupada and his movement. Actually these truths were never hidden! Prabhupada spoke these truths many many times and even in public lectures like in Vrndavana, September 16, 1976.

The world has come a long way since the 1970s and the effects of Prabhupada's preaching and the preaching of his sincere followers has brought a light into the darkness of this world. This light is manifesting as an awakening in the innocent people to the manipulation that they are being subjected to at the hands of the demoniac Jewish bankers. The fake moon landing, 911, World War 2 and the holohoax and the truth about Hitler are now more widely understood.

These people who are receiving Prabhupada's mercy due to their non envious hearts are awakening to truth. They are the REAL FUTURE of Prabhupada's Krishna Consciousness Movement!!!

These truth seekers see the current "ISKCON movement" for what it is, namely **a Jewish controlled den of blasphemy and deceit.** Now there is no bona fide ISKCON to give a bad name to! All we actually have left is TRUTH. And if we cannot speak truth NOW, we are lost and totally defeated as no truth seeker will take Prabhupada's message seriously!

The TRUE Krishna Consciousness Movement is very interested in TRUTHFULNESS. Truth is one of the divine qualities that the Lord mentions in Bhagavad-gita that men need to develop to come to the spiritual platform.

So it is time the world learns some real truths from Prabhupada directly in regards to the lies which the Jews [And Jewish Shills like Alex Jones] continue to propagate about Hitler and the First and Second World Wars. These lies have kept people as slaves for so many years. THESE TRUTHS WILL HELP THE INNOCENT PEOPLE OF THE WORLD BECOME FREE FROM THE JEWS DEMONIAC INFLUENCE IN THEIR LIVES AND BRING THEM INTO THE LIGHT OF PRABHUPADA'S SANKIRTANA MOVEMENT!

Prabhupada speaks of truth as follows:

> Satyam, truthfulness, means that facts should be presented as
> they are for the benefit of others. Facts should not be

misrepresented. According to social conventions, it is said that one can speak the truth only when it is palatable to others. But that is not truthfulness. The truth should be spoken in a straight and forward way, so that others will understand actually what the facts are. If a man is a thief and if people are warned that he is a thief, that is truth. Although sometimes the truth is unpalatable, one should not refrain from speaking it. Truthfulness demands that the facts be presented as they are for the benefit of others. That is the definition of truth. *[Bhagavad-gita As It Is (1972) 10.4-5]*

So we cannot refrain from speaking truth because some weak minded people who have had their consciousness deeply subverted by Jewish lies don't like to hear it. No, we cannot compromise. TRUTH SHOULD ALWAYS BE SPOKEN FOR THE BENEFIT OF ALL!

THE CONCLUSION:
Prabhupada never accepted the Jewish propaganda and lies about Hitler and the Holocaust.
NEITHER SHOULD YOU!!!

Adolf Hitler was chosen by Krishna to stop the spread of Jewish atheistic communism. This is a clear fact to anyone who has studied true history with their mind free from the subversion and lies told by the Jews. Why was Hitler used as the Lord's instrument? Because he had some qualification to be such an instrument as no ordinary person can be utilized by the Lord.

Prabhupada did not preach in Russia where the influence of the demoniac communism was strong. He preached in America and Europe where Christianity was still manifest to some degree and faith in Jesus the pure devotee could be freely expressed! This is what Hitler has fought to preserve!!! So how can anyone say that Hitler's fight was not divine? It directly assisted the Sankirtana Movement and preserved a field for preaching that the Lord knew he was going to send Srila Prabhupada into in 1965!!!!

"Lord God, give us the strength that we may retain our liberty for our children and our children's children, not only for ourselves but also for the other peoples of Europe, for this is a war which we all wage, this time, not for our German people alone, it is a war for all of Europe and with it, in the long run, for all of mankind." *[Adolf Hitler speech - Berlin, 30/01/ 1942]*

"My feelings as a Christian points me to my Lord and Savior as a fighter. It points me to the man who once in loneliness, surrounded only by a few followers, recognized these Jews for what they were and summoned men to fight against them and who, God's truth! was greatest not as a sufferer but as a fighter. In boundless love as a Christian and as a man I read through the passage which tells us how the Lord at last rose in His might and seized the scourge to drive out of the Temple the brood of vipers and adders. How terrific was His fight for the world against the Jewish poison. To-day, after two thousand years, with deepest emotion I recognize more profoundly than ever before in the fact that it was for this that He had to shed His blood upon the Cross. As a Christian I have no duty to allow myself to be cheated, but I have the duty to be a fighter for truth and justice…. And if there is anything which could demonstrate that we are acting rightly it is the distress that daily grows. For as a Christian I have also a duty to my own people." *[Adolf Hitler, in his speech in Munich on 12 April 1922]*

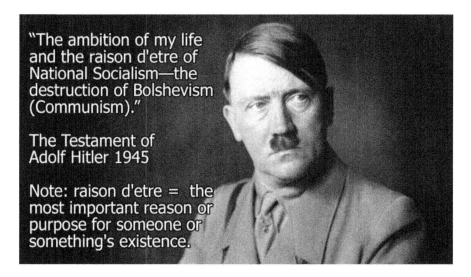

"The ambition of my life and the raison d'etre of National Socialism—the destruction of Bolshevism (Communism)."

The Testament of Adolf Hitler 1945

Note: raison d'etre = the most important reason or purpose for someone or something's existence.

NO TALK OF HITLER SAYS PRABHUPADA
BUT ONLY FOR THE FAITHLESS!

The following is a section from a Prabhupada letter which is misquoted by rascals to try to silence any discussion on Hitler:

Regarding Hitler, so Hitler may be good man or bad man, so what does he help to our Krishna Consciousness movement? But it is a fact that much propaganda was made against him, that much I know, and the Britishers are first-class propagandists. And I have heard that his officers did everything without informing him, just like in our ISKCON there are so many false things: "Prabhupada said this, Prabhupada said that." **But we have nothing to do with Hitler in our Krishna Consciousness. Do not be deviated by such ideas.** *[Prabhupada Letter to: Krishnadasa, Vrindaban, 7 November, 1972]*

This letter was clearly a time and place instruction to a doubting devotee. A devotee who struggled to believe in Prabhupada and his statements about the moon landing hoax and Hitler's true position as a good man, who didn't kill six million Jews. The letter was written shortly after Prabhupada's bombshell conversation about Hitler and the so called holocaust.

> Prabhupada: **He (Hitler) hesitated; therefore I don't believe that he killed so many Jews in concentration camps.**

SO THIS LETTER WAS NOT A 10,000 YEAR INSTRUCTION FOR ALL DEVOTEES, AS SOME RASCALS FALSELY TRY TO CLAIM. It was an instruction for a weak devotee with a disturbed mind, to help him claim back his faith in the words of his spiritual master. Note how Prabhupada again asserted the truth about Hitler to Krishnadasa in this letter:

> But it is a fact that much propaganda was made against him, that much I know, and the Britishers are first-class propagandists.

Please read the full letter below and see the context and before you do that, remember that Prabhupada said:

> **The Vedas instruct us that knowledge must always be considered in terms of desa-kala-patra.** Desa means "circumstances," kala means "time," and patra means "the object." We must understand everything by taking these three elements into consideration. *[Prabhupada Morning Walk April 18, 1973, In Cheviot Hills Park, Los Angeles.]*

So the misuse of this time, place and circumstance quote is only used by rascals to silence any use of Prabhupada numerous revolutionary statements about the true nature of Adolf Hitler. I am using them in my preaching to attract to Prabhupada's lotus feet all those numerous millions and millions of souls now awakened to the dangerous Jewish problem plaguing our world! TRYING TO CHECK THIS PREACHING IS AN ACT OF GROSS ENVY DUE TO HATRED OF ADOLF HITLER BY THOSE CONTAMINATED BY JEWISH LIES!

Prabhupada himself even utilised Hitler to promote his Bhagavad-gita at a time when nearly all the western world was asleep to Hitler's true nature. So how ludicrous is it to say we cannot use Prabhupada's truthful revelations about Hitler for all those millions of souls now awakened from the Jewish lies.

> **Hitler was a great student of Bhagavad-gita.** And there were many scholars still reading Bhagavad-gita, trying to understand. Just see what best depth of knowledge He has given. It is made by Krishna. So in knowledge, in wealth, in strength, in beauty, and in everything He was opulent. Therefore He is Bhagavan. You cannot accept any ordinary man as Bhagavan. *[Bhagavad-gita Lecture 2.7-11, New York, March 2, 1966]*

> **BHAGAVATA IS VERY OPEN FOR DISCUSSING ALL SUBJECT MATTER. WE SHOULD NOT HIDE ANYTHING ARTIFICIALLY. WE MUST DISCUSS THE FACT.**

> **So Srimad-Bhagavatam, everything threadbare discussed**, very practical, and Absolute Truth. There are social, political, religious. Everything is discussed very scientifically... In Chicago, when I was there, they talked about independence of the woman. They asked me question. So I replied, "No, woman cannot be given independence." So there was a great agitation against me. In many papers I was very much criticized. But actually it is the fact, because they are innocent, not so intelligent and... These are all practical. We may avoid discussing, **but Bhagavata is very open for discussing all subject matter. That is fact. We should not hide anything artificially. We must discuss the fact.** *[Prabhupada Lecture From Srimad-Bhagavatam 5.6.4,Vrndavana, November 26, 1976]*

Why should we hide the truths Prabhupada spoke about Adolf Hitler? Prabhupada says we shouldn't hide anything artificially. We must discuss the fact. We cannot present a time, place and circumstance letter that Srila Prabhupada wrote to a devotee lacking faith in the words of the spiritual master and use that letter as a 10,000 year gag order, to silence any discussion on Hitler and the Second World War. That is total rascaldom!

Of course in the 70s when the world was totally overwhelmed by untruths, Prabhupada didn't want disciples of his newly developing Hare Krishna movement in the west, to go shouting the facts he spoke about Hitler from the rooftops. Still if he didn't want them discussed and presented at a later date when the time was more favorable to these truths, he would never have spoken them at all. Prabhupada knew that the lies of International Jewry covering the consciousness of humanity would eventually be totally exposed due to the rising of the Golden Age. And he knew the truths he spoke about Hitler could be utilized to attract those awakened to the Jewish problem.

> Prabhupada: The earth was flat. They believed that the world is flat. So how much imperfect knowledge they have got. So imperfect knowledge, how long it can go? Just like we are going to challenge all these rascals that life is grown out of matter. We are going to challenge. It is not a fact. So how long you can cheat people? For hundred, two hundred, thousand years, but you cannot cheat for all the time.
> Umapati: It has been going on from time immemorial. I guess they figure they can just keep going on for time immemorial.
> Prabhupada: No time immemorial. You are being cheated for two hundred, three hundred years, that's all. Not before that. All these scientists rascals, have come out within two hundred years. That's all. **So you are being cheated for the last two hundred years, not for thousands of years. So it will be finished. Within another fifty years, everything will be finished.**
> Karandhara: Yes, they say now there is an anti-intellectual movement. People are rebelling to science and modern progress.
> Prabhupada: What is that science? That is not science. That is ignorance. Ignorance. Simply ignorance. Ignorance is going as science. Irreligion is going as religion. **So how long it will go? People are becoming intelligent.** [*Morning Walk At Cheviot Hills Golf Course, May 15, 1973, Los Angeles*]

We can see that this prediction by Srila Prabhupada has unfolded with 100% accuracy. The great awakening is here in 2023, fifty years after he called it. All the Jewish lies and cheating have been exposed. People are becoming spiritually intelligent, this is due to the age of Satya [Truth] inaugurated by Sri

Caitnaya Mahaprabhu.

Therefore those trying to say that to present the truths Prabhupada spoke about Hitler will give a bad name to His Divine Grace or the Krishna Consciousness movement are either totally asleep about true world history or are working on the side of communism for the demons.

ISKCON is now totally controlled by International Jewry, how can it be given a bad name? It already has a bad name in the eyes of any pious souls who see through the façade. The best way to defend Prabhupada from blasphemy is not to pamper to liberals who are simply soft communists totally against real God consciousness, but to present Prabhupada's revolutionary statements on all topics to those who are awakened from Jewish lies. They are the best recipients for the absolute truths of the Vedas, not envious communists who are the greatest enemies of Prabhupada and Aryan culture.

PRABHUPADA'S LETTER IN FULL TO
A DISTURBED AND DOUBTFUL KRISHNADASA

Letter to: Krishnadasa, Vrindaban, 7 November, 1972

My Dear Krishnadasa,

Please accept my blessings. I beg to acknowledge receipt of your letter dated October 30, 1972, and I have noted the contents. **It appears that you are again constantly disturbed by the same nonsense doubts.** These things are not very important, we may not waste our time with these insignificant questions. If we are seeking to find out some fault, maya will give us all facility to find any small thing and make it very big, that is maya. But such questions as yours: why there is so-called discrepancy between the views of Bhagavat and modern scientists regarding the moon and other planets, and whether Hitler is good or bad man, these are most insignificant matters, and for anyone who is sincerely convinced that Krishna is the Supreme Personality of Godhead, for him these questions do not arise. Our information comes from Vedas, and if we believe Krishna, that

vedaham samatitani
vartamanani carjuna
bhavisyani ca bhutani

mam tu veda na kascana
(BG, VII, 26)

that He knows everything, and "vedais ca sarvair aham eva
vedyo vedanta-krd veda-vid eva caham," that Krishna is non-
different from Vedas, then these questions do not arise.
But because you have asked me, I am your spiritual master, I
must try to answer to your satisfaction. Yes, sometimes in
Vedas such things like the asura's decapitated head chasing
after Candraloka, sometimes it is explained allegorically. Just
like now we are explaining in 4th Canto of Srimad-Bhagavatam
the story of King Puranjana. Just like the living entity is living
within this body, and the body is described there as city with
nine gates, the intelligence as the Queen. So there are
sometimes allegorical explanations. So there are many things
which do not corroborate with the so-called modern science,
because they are explained in that way. But where is the
guarantee that modern science is also correct? So we are
concerned with Krishna Consciousness, and even though there
is some difference of opinion between modern science and
allegorical explanation in the Bhagavat, we have to take the
essence of Srimad-Bhagavatam and utilize it for our higher
benefit, without bothering about the correctness of the modern
science or the allegorical explanation sometimes made in
Srimad-Bhagavatam. But this is a fact that in each and every
planet there is a predominant deity, as we have got experience
in this planet there is a president, so it is not wonderful when
the predominating deity fights with another predominating deity
of another planet. The modern science takes everything as dead
stone. We take it for granted that everything is being
manipulated by a person in each and every affair of the
cosmology. The modern scientists however could not make any
progress in the understanding of the Supreme Personality of
Godhead, therefore we do not accept modern science as very
perfect. We take Krishna's version:

gam avisya ca bhutani
dharayamy aham ojasa
pusnami causadhih sarvah
somo bhutvah rasatmakah
(BG, 15.13)

"I become the moon," and "yac chandramasi yac cagnau," (ibid,
12) "I am the splendor of the moon," and "jyotisam api taj
jyotis," (BG, 13.18) "I am the source of light in all luminous

objects," so no one is able to give us the correct information than Krishna, that you should know

Regarding Hitler, so Hitler may be good man or bad man, so what does he help to our Krishna Consciousness movement? But it is a fact that much propaganda was made against him, that much I know, and the Britishers are first-class propagandists. And I have heard that his officers did everything without informing him, just like in our ISKCON there are so many false things: "Prabhupada said this, Prabhupada said that." But we have nothing to do with Hitler in our Krishna Consciousness. Do not be deviated by such ideas "Jnanam jneyam jnana-gamyam," (ibid), Krishna is knowledge, He is the object of knowledge, He is the goal of knowledge, and

> you mam evam asammudho
> janati purusottamam
> sa sarva-vid bhajati mam
> (BG, XV, 19)

"Whoever knows Me as the Supreme Personality of Godhead, without doubting, is to be understood as the knower of everything, and he engages himself therefore in devotional service"–this is the understanding of advanced devotee, so my best advice to you is to agree to come to this understanding.

Your ever well-wisher, A. C. Bhaktivedanta Swami

Conclusion: Those who like to misquote the above letter to silence any discussions on Adolf Hitler are clearly in the same category as Krishnadasa. They are doubtful souls who have no faith in the words of Srila Prabhupada. Now their cheating has being exposed.

DID PRABHUPADA SAY HITLER
WAS A SAKTYAVESA-AVATARA?

In this article I will establish with Prabhupada's direct quotes that Hitler was a saktyavesa-avatara specifically empowered to cut down rogues and demons namely Jewish Bolshevism.

There is a video of Hamsaduta dasa talking about his memories of Prabhupada. In one of them he relates a discussion he had with Srila Prabhupada about Hitler:

> Hamsaduta dasa: And another time he said Hitler was a saktyavesa-avatara. I said a saktyavesa-avatara? Yes he said. He said saktyavesa-avatara means one who descends with special power, who is empowered to do something. It doesn't mean, saktyavesa-avatara doesn't mean he always does good but he may also do destructive things.

I recently made a post on Facebook which also touches on this topic:

> The main point is that Hitler Protected and saved Europe. The Lord empowered him for that purpose so the west would be saved for Prabhupada!!! **That's why Prabhupada says he was a saktyavesa-avatara EMPOWERED TO DESTROY THE JEWISH BOLSHEVIKS!!!** Only the most fallen degraded and totally deluded so called followers of Prabhupada cannot see

this! They don't realize that if it wasn't for Hitler and the Waffen SS then we would all have been living in a communist Russia or China like situation since around 1940 and getting shot if we even chanted Hare Krishna in our own homes!!! Surely we should have a little appreciation for Hitler and the Waffen SS and their brave sacrifice.

For me Hitler's position as an empowered soul is a no-brainer. It only requires that one has a basic understanding of the true history in regards to the First and Second World Wars and a little common sense. But for those deluded souls bewildered by Jewish lies it will be difficult to comprehend the obvious truth.

The Jews plans for world domination are clearly described in their Protocols of the Learned Elders of Zion. The brutality they inflicted upon the people of Russia in fulfilment of those plans was heading towards all of Europe and the rest of the world. Hitler fought valiantly to protect the west from this demoniac onslaught. Considering Germany's position after World War One, this miraculous fight against Jewish world domination could only have been possible for an empowered personality.

Adolf Hitler did great things to build up his own country, amazing feats unprecedented in history. He picked up all the people in Germany from the depths of despair after the First World War and the cruel Treaty of Versailles. He built his nation up and made it a world superpower. He kicked out international Jewry, kicked out the bankers and built up his nation, got everybody employed, got the country thriving, giving all the people a beautiful way of life, the best civilization in modern history. Everybody was happy and joyous and that's why they worshiped Hitler. The German people are highly intelligent and they worshiped Hitler because they knew he loved them and he was taking care of them like a true leader and a true King should do.

So when one can see all these truths about Hitler and understand that communism or the Bolshevik revolution was factually controlled by Jews then one can appreciate Hitler's great efforts to check them, against all odds. Germany was more or less on her own in the great fight, with only Italy and Japan giving support along with Finland etc. But in reality it was mainly Germany alone that stood up against the might of international Jewry who controlled Russia, America, England and France.

Anybody who can just study a little history can understand that Hitler was especially empowered. It's just so obvious he was empowered to destroy the Bolsheviks. Why is that you may ask? Well Krishna in his form of Caitanya Mahaprabhu has His plan to deliver all the conditioned souls. He predicted that in every town and village of the world the Lord will be glorified. The Lord sent his pure devotee Srila Prabhupada to the west to fulfil this great prophecy. Therefore to protect that preaching field for Prabhupada, he empowered Hitler to protect it. I have made this point many times before and it is so clear to those with common sense. Yet these deluded mind controlled so called devotees, cannot see this obvious truth.

Well I'm going to prove directly from Prabhupada's teachings that Hitler was empowered or a saktyavesa-avatara.

So I got this message from Mahesh dasa in which he quotes me and responds:

> Mahesh Dasa: "That's why Prabhupada says he was saktyavesa-avatara EMPOWERED TO DESTROY THE JEWISH BOLSHEVIKS!!!" I have not come across that. Search on this https://prabhupadabooks.com/. There is nothing. Where does Srila Prabhupada say this?

So he has put his challenge to me, and that is fair enough. He's probably realizing that Prabhupada said this to Hamsaduta. So he is going present the following quote to me in regards to the authority of Hamsaduta's statement:

> My Dear Omkara dasi: Please accept my blessings. I have seen your letter dated August 17, 1975 and have noted the contents. I never said there should be no more marriage. By all means legally you can get married. How can I object? They misunderstand me. **Unless it is there from me in writing, there are so many things that "Prabhupada said."**
> *[Prabhupada Letter to: Omkara Vrindaban 2 September, 1975]*

So basically Mahesh will say that unless it's in writing, or there is a recording of Prabhupada saying this, then there are so many things that Prabhupada supposedly said, so how can we accept it? We won't accept it just because Hamsaduta says it, there are so many things that "Prabhupada said". Anybody can say Prabhupada said this to me, Prabhupada said that to me, so that's a fair comment and the correct position to hold.

So what I'm going to do in this article is prove that Hitler was a saktyavesa-avatara with Prabhupada's direct statements. When I do that, then Hamsaduta's memory of Prabhupada saying Hitler was saktyavesa-avatara who descended to do destruction, (which is obviously his fight to stop this Bolshevik revolution) will be given full power and support. Then it will no longer be in the realm of hearsay, it will be completely supported as if

Prabhupada has said it directly.

Another thing the sceptics will say about Hamsaduta to refute his testimony about Hitler will be as follows: "He was a bogus guru, he fell down and he was a deviant so how can he be trusted?" But the one thing I will say in regards to Hamsaduta is that he was the only person other than maybe Locannatha who was actually trying to get Prabhupada out of the room in Vrindavan when he was being poisoned.

Prabhupada had requested to be taken from his room in 1977 for Bullock Cart Parikrama. Prabhupada wanted to be taken out of the room into the fresh air and the sunlight with his real disciples, where he said he would recover his health and finish the Bhagavatam. Hamsaduta had faith in that instruction given by Prabhupada and tried to execute the order even though the demons headed by Tamal Krishna were against that order and they were pushing in the other way to keep Prabhupada in his room so they could kill him. At least Hamsaduta stood up for Prabhupada and tried to take him on bullock cart. Ultimately he wasn't successful but he made an effort, he showed some desire to save Prabhupada.

Later he got taken in by these demons, he got bewildered and he went along with their deviations, such as the bogus guru system in ISKCON. So that's not good, I am not condoning that, but at least later on he tried to rectify that by admitting the truth that Prabhupada had never appointed them gurus but only ritvik priests. Obviously he didn't have enough strength and courage to actually admit that Prabhupada was actually poisoned because that would be a difficult thing for him to say. Because he would basically have to face the fact that he didn't save Prabhupada from being killed, that would be a hard bitter pill for him to swallow, something very difficult for him to bear.

I've even seen a reverse speech from Brahmananda and in his subconscious mind he said or communicated to Prabhupada "I'd like to help you but I need a rope." So there's nothing hidden in the subtle plane, everybody who was in that room in Vrindavana or around Prabhupada at that time, knew he was being poisoned, they all knew it but they were afraid to do anything about it. Hamsaduta did try to do something about it! After he fell down to the position of the rest of the devotees by following Tamal and going along with his bogus guru system, but in the end he actually came clean and spoke the truth about the guru issue.

Let us look at some of Prabhupada's statements on saktyavesha-avatara:

> TRANSLATION: Sri Caitanya Mahaprabhu replied, "O Sanatana, you must give up your intelligent tricks. Just try to

understand the meaning of the saktyavesa-avatara.

TRANSLATION: "There are unlimited saktyavesa-avataras of Lord Krishna. Let Me describe the chief among them.

TRANSLATION: "Empowered incarnations are of two types– primary and secondary. The primary one is directly empowered by the Supreme Personality of Godhead and is called an incarnation. **The secondary one is indirectly empowered by the Supreme Personality of Godhead and is called vibhuti.**

TRANSLATION: "Some saktyavesa-avataras are the four Kumaras, Narada, Maharaja Prthu and Parasurama. When a living being is empowered to act as Lord Brahma, he is also considered a saktyavesa-avatara.

TRANSLATION: "Lord Sesa in the spiritual world of Vaikuntha and, in the material world, Lord Ananta, who carries innumerable planets on His hood, are two primary empowered incarnations. There is no need to count the others, **for they are unlimited.**

TRANSLATION: "The power of knowledge was invested in the four Kumaras, and the power of devotional service was invested in Narada. The power of creation was invested in Lord Brahma, and the power to carry innumerable planets was invested in Lord Ananta.

TRANSLATION: "The Supreme Personality of Godhead invested the power of personal service to Lord Sesa, and He invested the power to rule the earth in King Prthu. **Lord Parasurama received the power to kill rogues and miscreants.**

PURPORT: Krishna says in Bhagavad-gita (Bg. 4.8): paritranaya sadhunam vinasaya ca duskrtam. Sometimes the Lord invests His power to rule in a king like Prthu **and enables such a king to kill rogues and miscreants. He also invests His power in incarnations like Parasurama.**

TRANSLATION: " **'Whenever the Lord is present in someone by portions of His various potencies, the living entity representing the Lord is called saktyavesa-avatara–**

that is, an incarnation invested with special power.'

PURPORT: This verse is found in the Laghu-bhagavatamrta (1.18).

TRANSLATION: "As explained in the Eleventh Chapter of Bhagavad-gita, Krishna has spread Himself all over the universe **in many personalities through specific powers, known as vibhuti.**

PURPORT: The expansion of specific maya powers is explained in Srimad-Bhagavatam (2.7.39). *[Prabhupada from Caitanya Caritamrta Madhya Lila 20-366 to 374]*

These are the symptoms by which we can understand that he's also saktyavesa avatara. And the Bhagavad-gita you'll find, yad yad vibhutimat sattvam mama tejo-'msa-sambhavam. Anyone, not only Lord Buddha or others, but anyone, Lord, in the Bhagavad-gita it is stated, **anyone who has got some extraordinary power, uncommon power, he's to be considered vibhu. Saktyavesa avatara, there are two kinds, one directly empowered for particular mission, comes from the transcendental spiritual sky, and others, those who are in this material world, but they have got some specific power, uncommon power, not found in ordinary man. They are called vibhuti.** This vibhuti (is) explained in the Bhagavad-gita: yad yad vibhutimat sattvam mama tejo-'msa sambhavam.......

Parasurame 'dusta-nasaka-virya-sancarana' Parasurama... Paritranaya sadhunam vinasaya ca duskrtam. Under two, these two missions, the Lord comes, incarnates, descends. And Parasurama was supposed to kill the dusta, the wicked ksatriyas, when they forgot to rule over the world as bona fide ksatriyas. They..., they..., they were killed twenty-one times, and it is mentioned in the Mahabharata during that killing process, many ksatriyas fled from, fled away from India and they settled in other parts of the world, especially in Europe. It is mentioned in the Mahabharata. So Parasurama was especially meant, vinasaya ca duskrtam, to kill the miscreants.......

Another definition is given by Sanatana Gosvami. This same Sanatana Gosvami who is now being taught by Lord Caitanya, he also has written many books. These two brothers, Rupa

Gosvami and Sanatana Gosvami, and their nephew, Jiva Gosvami, composed many valuable literatures. So Sanatana Gosvami has written one book, Laghu-bhagavatamrtam. Laghu-bhagavatamrtam, supplementary to Srimad-Bhagavatam. So in that Laghu-bhagavatamrtam book, he has written,

> jnana-saktya-adi-kalaya
> yatravisto janardanah
> ta avesa nigadyante
> jiva eva mahattamah

He has defined that these saktyavesa avatara, they are all living entities; they are not on the level of Visnu-tattva. But they have special power and special, I mean to say, opulence to glorify the Supreme Lord.

> 'vibhuti' kahiye yaiche gita-ekadase
> jagat vyapila Krishna-sakty-abhasavese

Now that vibhuti is, is mentioned by Lord Caitanya. That vibhutimat sattvam, saktyavesa, there are many, many... We find in the history so many extraordinary, powerful men come and go. They are called vibhuti of the Supreme Lord.

> yad yad vibhutimat sattvam
> srimad urjitam eva va
> tat tad evavagaccha tvam
> mama tejo-'msa-sambhavam

Anyone extraordinary. You'll be, I mean to..., pleased to learn that in India, the king is considered vibhutimat sattvam. King. He is also considered as the incarnation of God, king. [*Prabhupada Lecture: Sri Caitanya-caritamrta, Madhya-lila 20.367-84, New York, December 31, 1966*]

So this is the category of incarnation that Adolf Hitler belongs to. Prabhupada says above:

Anyone who has got some extraordinary power, uncommon power, he's to be considered vibhu. Saktyavesa avatara, there are two kinds, one directly empowered for particular mission, comes from the transcendental spiritual sky, and others, those who are in this material world, but they have got some specific power, uncommon power, not found in ordinary man. They are called vibhuti.

When Prabhupada told Hamsaduta that Hitler was a saktyavesa-avatara who descended to do destruction, this is vibhuti. Hitler would have been a demigod given special power uncommon power this is clear. We shall look further on at other quotes for those who cannot use logic and reason to see what Hitler did and understand that he did uncommon things that no ordinary man could have done, like lifting Germany from the depths of despair, fighting against international Jewry, checking them from taking over the rest of the world and destroying it and making it a completely Godless place. Hitler had uncommon power to check this demoniac attack, if people can't understand this fact with logic and reason by studying true history, then I will show some direct quotes from Srila Prabhupada where he does say that Hitler had great power, extraordinary power. So Hitler he's in the category of vibhuti, he is in the material world, a demigod and he was giving a specific power, uncommon power not found in an ordinary man.

Prabhupada said above:

> Now that vibhuti is, is mentioned by Lord Caitanya. That vibhutimat sattvam, saktyavesa, there are many, many... We find in the history so many extraordinary, powerful men come and go. They are called vibhuti of the Supreme Lord.

This is again proof that Hitler was in the category of vibhuti, especially empowered, but Hitler wasn't just like any ordinary great man in this world he fought against the demons to protect the west for Prabhupada.

> Anyone extraordinary. You'll be, I mean to..., pleased to learn that in India, the king is considered vibhutimat sattvam. King. He is also considered as the incarnation of God, king.

Hitler is the closest thing we have had in modern times to an incarnation in the mood of a king. The king is considered to be the incarnation of God, so Hitler was the closest thing to Vedic king we have had in recent times because he ruled his citizens in the spirit of a Vedic king. He gave the people in Germany a great way of life, free from debt slavery and he had spiritual goals for his nation.

The Third Reich was in contact with the Gaudiya Math, they had the Vedic literatures and there were even plans for teaching vaisnavism in German universities. As I quoted previously Prabhupada said Hitler was so much fond of Vedic civilization, (meaning he was fond of Krishna) so much so that he marked his flag with a swastika and he was a great student of the Bhagavad-gita, which is the book taught to the Vedic kings.

Hitler wasn't even in this category of just an extra ordinary powerful man who come and go in the material world, he was specifically empowered to protect the sankirtan movement of Lord Caitanya because the demons, who are not even from this planet, are looking to take over the earth. We are going to look into that later, we will look at Govinda dasi's memory which the rascals will also challenge and say that's just a memory of hers, and so it's not true. But again I can also support that memory with direct quotes from Srila Prabhupada later.

> Martin: You, you say that… (break) …who created this
> knowledge that this flower and the banyan tree is Krishna. What
> place in the divine scheme do such great names as Buddha,
> Jesus, Muhammad have?
> Prabhupada: Yes. Buddha, we accept him as incarnation, as
> expansion of Krishna. He's Krishna working as Buddha, Lord
> Buddha. Kesava dhrta buddha sarira. He has accepted body of
> Buddha. That is our conception of Lord Buddha.
> Martin: And Jesus Christ and Muhammad?
> Prabhupada: Everyone.
> Martin: They were all the reincarnation of Krishna?
> Prabhupada: Yes.
> Martin: I see.
> Prabhupada: **Yad yad vibhuti. Any, anyone who is showing**
> **some extraordinary power, he is supposed to be incarnation**
> **of Krishna's energy. Yad yad vibhutimat sattvam mama**
> **tejo 'msa-sambhavam. The brilliant energy. He represents**
> **the brilliant energy of Krishna. And the energy is not**
> **different from the energetic.** [May Room Conversation,
> Mexico, May 4, 1972]

Hitler was given the power of Krishna and that power of Krishna is not different than Krishna, and that is why he is a saktyavesa-avatara in the vibhuti category. Adolf Hitler was most definitely a saktyavesa-avatara and what was his business? That we will see in the next quote.

> The saktyavesa-avatara is categorized into (1) forms of divine
> absorption (bhagavad-avesa) like Kapiladeva or Rsabhadeva
> and (2) divinely empowered forms (saktyavesa), of whom there
> are seven: (1) Sesa Naga in the Vaikuntha world, empowered
> for the personal service of the Supreme Lord (sva-sevana-sakti),
> (2) Anantadeva, empowered to bear all the planets within the

universe (bhu-dharana-sakti), (3) Lord Brahma, empowered with the energy to create the cosmic manifestation (srsti-sakti), (4) Catuhsana, or the Kumaras, specifically empowered to distribute transcendental knowledge (jnana-sakti), (5) Narada Muni, empowered to distribute devotional service (bhakti-sakti), (6) Maharaja Prthu, specifically empowered to rule and maintain the living entities (palana-sakti) and (7) **Parasurama, specifically empowered to cut down rogues and demons (dusta-damana-sakti).** [Sri Caitanya-caritamrta – 1975 Cc. Madhya-lila 20.246]

When Prabhupada told Hamsaduta that Hitler was empowered to do destructive things, we can understand from the above quote what that destruction was. It would fall into the category of dusta-damana-sakti. Hitler was a saktyavesa-avatara specifically empowered to cut down rogues and demons, namely the Godless Jewish Bolsheviks.

Hitler was empowered to cut down the Jewish Bolsheviks so they weren't able to take over the whole world and inflict their brutal torture on all of humanity. They were not successful in their endeavour for world domination because Adolf Hitler cut them down! After the Second World War from the Berlin wall right through to America the western world was relatively free thanks to Adolf Hitler and the brave soldiers of Waffen-SS.

From then the demons have worked with a silent war, a war of manipulation behind the scenes demoralising the west with their cultural Marxist revolution. Still Hitler's fight had kept the west free enough for Prabhupada to come and openly spread Krishna Consciousness because America still had constitutional freedom of religion. Everywhere in the Western world Prabhupada could preach Krishna Consciousness unimpeded. No such freedoms were available in the communist countries controlled by international Jewry. Prabhupada said that in communist China people would even be killed for chanting Hare Krishna in their own homes and in Russia they would take you away to some unknown place like Siberia.

Wherever international Jewry through their communist Bolshevik revolution has taken control, there you will find tyranny, where no one is allowed to be God conscious. So how would Prabhupada be able to preach under such conditions? One may say that Prabhupada can do anything, he is a pure devotee. Yes, Prabhupada could even fly to America as he has mystic power; still he sailed on the Jaladuta. So in the same way if Krishna wants to protect the west so Prabhupada can go there and nicely preach Krishna Consciousness, in a favourable field, then he needs to empower someone to cut down the demons who are trying to make that implausible. The demons have an agenda to rule the world and they have already taken Russia, now they're coming across to conquer the rest of the world. So what's Krishna going to do? He's obviously going to send somebody down with special powers to cut them down, DUSTA-DAMANA-SAKTI!!! So that personality was Adolf Hitler. So when we look at Prabhupada's teachings correctly, we can see that Hitler is in this category of being especially empowered to cut down rogues and demons.

Some people will say "We don't see Prabhupada talking directly about Hitler's uncommon activities." They are such rascals! They will all say that they can only accept things if Prabhupada says it directly. They can't use their brains and follow Prabhupada's definitions and look at history and judge a man to see if he has got extraordinary power and uncommon activities. One has to use common sense and judge if Hitler had some extraordinary power. Analyse and use your brain. It's not that Prabhupada has to spoon feed you everything! Still for those who like to be spoon fed, I will give you some nice spoon feeding. Look at these quotes:

> An example can help us to understand the **inconceivable potency of the Supreme Lord. In the recent history of warfare the Supreme Personality of Godhead created a Hitler and, before that, a Napoleon Bonaparte, and they each killed many living entities in war**. But in the end Bonaparte and Hitler were also killed. People are still very much interested in writing and reading books about Hitler and Bonaparte and how they killed so many people in war. Year after year many books are published for public reading regarding **Hitler's killing thousands of Jews in confinement. (NOT SIX MILLION!!!!)** But no one is researching who killed Hitler and who created such a gigantic killer of human beings. *[Prabhupada From Srimad Bhagavatam 4.11.19]*

Napoleon also fought against international Jewry and their demoniac plans and Prabhupada says he and Hitler both killed many living entities in war (not in concentration camps). Hitler didn't kill millions in camps, he killed thousands of communist traitors that he put in confinement. This practice is standard for all traitors who work to destroy a country from within. So this is also Prabhupada again confirming what he had discussed in the morning walk from 1972:

Prabhupada: **He (Hitler) hesitated; therefore I don't believe that he killed so many Jews in concentration camps.**

Again from the pages of Srimad Bhagavatam in plain sight, Prabhupada is denying the holocaust for all those who have the ears to hear it. I had made other videos and documentaries on this topic.

So if those people out there can't use their God-given intelligence to judge if Hitler had some uncommon activities and extraordinary power, which would show us that he was vibhuti, empowered saktyavesa-avatara, then here is a direct quote from Prabhupada saying that Krishna created him as a gigantic killer of human beings in war. That war was not the war described to us by the Jews and their mind control media. Hitler was a gigantic killer of those rogues and demons who actually want to take over the world. He was empowered by the Lord to cut them down and kill them. He was created by Krishna's inconceivable potency. That is why he is a saktyavesa-avatara.

> In each body the living entity performs so many acts. Sometimes he becomes a great hero–just like Hiranyakasipu and Kamsa **or, in the modern age, Napoleon or Hitler. The activities of such men are certainly very great,** but as soon as their bodies are finished, everything else is finished. *[Prabhupada From Bhagavatam 4.25.10]*

> **Such a great, powerful man like Napoleon, Hitler**, they struggled only. Later on, they vanquished. So what to speak of others? Such big, big men, they struggled against the nature, but they vanquished. Nature is there. Nature is always victorious. So we have to own over victory over the nature. That is only possible if you take shelter of Krishna. *[Room Conversation with Anna Conan Doyle, daughter-in-law of famous author, Sir Arthur Conan Doyle August 10, 1973, Paris]*

Here again we see Prabhupada saying Hitler is a powerful man and his activities are certainly very great. This is another direct quote confirming his position as saktyavesa-avatara in the vibhuti category.

MAHESH RESPONDS

After I replied to Mahesh's challenge in regards to Hitler being a saktyavesa-avatara he responed with the following quote:

> Prabhupada: Yad yad vibhutimat sattva. Anyone a sense of exceptional qualities, mama tejo'amsa-sambhavam [Bg 10.41], Krishna says, "They are born of my tejah, amsa."

> [Know that all beautiful, glorious, and mighty creations spring from but a spark of My splendor.]

But that does not mean he is incarnation. There were many persons, **Hitler was also a very big man but that does not mean he becomes an incarnation**. Napoleon Bonaparte, he also was a very big man. So in this world you will find big and bigger, bigger, bigger. One is bigger than another then up to go to Brahma. Who can become like Brahma? He has created this whole universe and he lives, you know? He lives: sahasra-yuga-paryantam, ahar yad brahmano viduh [Bg 8.17], you can not calculate even his one day's life. *(710222SB-GORAKHPUR)*

This is actually a great quote that Mahesh has found which proves that Hitler is not an ordinary man but vibhuti... he is not a primary incarnation, he is secondary:

TRANSLATION: "There are unlimited saktyavesa-avataras of Lord Krishna. Let Me describe the chief among them.

TRANSLATION: "Empowered incarnations are of two types–primary and secondary. The primary one is directly empowered by the Supreme Personality of Godhead and is called an incarnation. **The secondary one is indirectly empowered by the Supreme Personality of Godhead and is called vibhuti.** *[Prabhupada from Caitanya Caritamrta Madhya Lila 20-367-8]*

Hitler is not directly Krishna, and never claimed to be like Ramakrishna did, which is what this conversation quoted by Mahesh is about. (the actually context, see the full quote below) Still Hitler was empowered (vibhuti - secondary empowered incarnation) to destroy the Bolsheviks to protect the west for Prabhupada. That is clear fact for anyone who knows true history. AND THE TEST TO PROVE IT!!!

TRANSLATION: Know that all beautiful, glorious, and mighty creations spring from but a spark of My splendor.

PURPORT: Any glorious or beautiful existence should be understood to be but **a fragmental manifestation of Krishna's opulence, whether it be in the spiritual or material world. <u>Anything extraordinarily opulent should be considered to represent Krishna's opulence.</u>** *[Bhagavd-gita 10.41]*

MAHESH QUOTE WITH THE FULL CONTEXT

Prabhupada: He may be, a person **may be very great devotee**, great man, that is another thing. **But to accept one as incarnation, that is different.**

Indian Guest: [indistinct]

Prabhupada: Yes. He may be very great man, that is alright.

Indian Guest: [indistinct]

Prabhupada: **Yad yad vibhutimat sattva. Anyone a sense of exceptional qualities, mama tejo'amsa-sambhavam [Bg 10.41], Krishna says, "They are born of my tejah, amsa."**

[Know that all beautiful, glorious, and mighty creations spring from but a spark of My splendor.]

But that does not mean he is incarnation. **There were many persons, Hitler was also a very big man but that does not mean he becomes an incarnation.** Napoleon Bonaparte, he also was a very big man. So in this world you will find big and bigger, bigger, bigger. One is bigger than another then up to go to Brahma. Who can become like Brahma? He has created this whole universe and he lives, you know? He lives: sahasra-yuga-paryantam, ahar yad brahmano viduh [Bg 8.17], you can not calculate even his one day's life.

[By human calculation, a thousand ages taken together is the duration of Brahma's one day. And such also is the duration of his night.]

But he's not, he never says that, "I am incarnation and God." So powerful. In comparison to Brahma what are these insignificant—insignificant creatures? He is creator of this universe and his one day's life you can not calculate, that is stated in the Bhagavad-gita: sahasra-yuga-paryantam. Forty-three lahks of years makes one yuga and multiply it by thousand, sahasra yuga ahar yad, that is Brahma's twelve hours period. **But he has never claims that he is incarnation of God. And what to speak of these insignificant—insignificant persons.** So God or God's incarnation not so cheap thing? You should know what is God. That's from Bhagavad-gita straight line [?], this Brahma, why twelve hours you cannot calculate? And how many in three days? Twelve hours you can calculate but twelve hours, again twelve hours night. Then, sahasra-yuga-paryantam, again in this one month, and this in one year, such one thousand years, a one hundred years to be. So you can not calculate. **Such a big personality, the first-born creature within this universe, he also never claims that, "I am incarnation of God."**

Indian Guest: [indistinct] Ramakrishna, he never would have claimed [indistinct]

Prabhupada: Yes, yes. He, he claimed, he claimed. He claimed he said that, "I am the same Rama and Krishna and Vivekananda accepted it."

Indian Guest: [indistinct]

Prabhupada: That way, that means he claimed, he claimed. If he did not claim then how Vivekananda knew that he is incarnation? Well, at the last moment you can also say. Does it mean, does it, does it prove that you are incarnation? We shall have to see, what are your symptoms of incarnation. That is stated in this. Just like characteristics, if you want to test one, any chemical, say test this salt. The salt and the sugar, it is looking the same, sometimes we mistake. By tasting we can know that this is salt and this is sugar. So what is the test? Simply by declaring somehow, "I am the same Krishna," also I become incarnation? What is the test? Just like test regarding Caitanya Mahaprabhu, Lord Buddhadeva, Kalki, there are tests. Lord Krishna, there is test, Lord Ramacandra, there is test. What is the test of this Ramakrishna becoming incarnation? *(710222SB-GORAKHPUR)*

So Hitler passed the test for a saktyavesa-avatara by showing extraordinary power in fighting against Jewish communism and protecting the west for Prabhupada.

BEAR-LIKE RACE OF BEINGS PROMOTING COMMUNISM DETERMINED TO CONVERT THE WORLD TO GODLESSNESS

In the next quote from Mother Govinda dasi we get to understand more clearly the true goals of communism and the identity of those who are actually behind it. This will help us to appreciate the fact that it couldn't be any ordinary man who would be able to fight against such powerful and demoniac personalities. It would require a special soul empowered by God. That man was Adolf Hitler.

> Srila Prabhupada sometimes said that a "bear-like race of beings had come from a lower planetary system, and were attempting to take over the Earth planet." This bear-like race of asuras had established themselves in Russia. And by promoting communism, a form of atheism, they were determined to convert the world to Godlessness.

> Formerly, in Vedic times, the land of Russia was known as the land of the rishis. It was known as "Rishiya." The region was populated by many yogis and sadhus who went to the mountains of the Himalayas, and beyond, to perform penances and austerities in the frozen terrain, far away from the hubbub of worldly life.

> Srila Prabhupada knew that there were those in Russia who were the descendants of such rishis, and would have the sukriti to take mightily to Krishna consciousness. Yet they were being suppressed and even tortured by the Godless asuric race that had overtaken the political systems of Russia.

> Those same asuric leaders were also keen on overtaking the political systems of other countries, closing their churches, and poisoning their children with government schools that taught only Darwinism, and other forms of atheism. In this way, the communist political machine planned to permeate the world with the poison of atheism. This was a serious threat to the future of the Earth planet.

> Srila Prabhupada often expressed concern for Russia, and for the suffering people there. It was almost as if he were tuned in to the sufferings of the saintly people in that iron-clad country. Because of the "iron curtain" as it was called, practically no interaction with the West was allowed. The "iron curtain" was firmly in place after World War II and anyone who tried to escape to the West, could be shot at various checkpoints. The asuras had successfully sealed off an entire country from the influence of the rest of the world, and were busily indoctrinating the helpless citizens with brutish atheism. (Govinda Dasi)

Now we are again going to face the same opposition to the above quote from Mother Govinda dasi as we faced for Hamsaduta's quote.

> **Unless it is there from me in writing, there are so many things that "Prabhupada said."** *[Prabhupada Letter to: Omkara Vrindaban 2 September, 1975]*

So can it be showed from Prabhupada's teachings that the people now trying to control our world are not even from this planet, that they are demons from a lower planetary system?

Let us look at a quote I presented before:

> The fight between the Lord, the Supreme Personality of Godhead, and the demon is compared to a fight between bulls for the sake of a cow. The earth planet is also called go, or cow. As bulls fight between themselves to ascertain who will have union with a cow, **there is always a constant fight between the demons and the Supreme Lord or His representative for supremacy over the earth**. *[Srila Prabhupada from Srimad Bhagavatam 3.18.20]*

So this quote is from the pastimes of the Lord in His incarnation as Varahadeva during His fight with the demon Hiranyaksa. Prabhupada says that always there is a constant fight for supremacy over the earth between the demons and the Supreme Lord or His representative.

Early in the same chapter we hear Hiranyaksa speak as follows:

> The demon addressed the Lord: O best of the demigods, dressed in the form of a boar, just hear me. **This earth is entrusted to us, the inhabitants of the lower regions,** and You cannot take it from my presence and not be hurt by me. *[Srimad Bhagavatam 3.18.3]*

Thus we see that the fight for earth is between the demons of the lower regions or lower planetary system and the Lord or His representatives. **This is a constant fight which is playing out even now. This is the clear proof which validates Mother Govinda Dasi's quote.**

There is this fight for mother earth between the demons and the Supreme Lord or His representative due to the fact that the earth is the field of activities for the spirit souls. On the other planets in the universe the souls are burning down their karmic reactions but on the earth the souls are making fresh karma which will determine their futures.

> After one enjoys the results of virtuous activities in the upper planetary systems, he comes down to this earth and renews his karma, or fruitive activities for promotion. This planet of human beings is considered the field of activities. *(Prabhupada from Bhagavad-gita 15.2)*

From the earth one can attain any planet in the universe, or if he desires he can go beyond that as described by the Lord in Bhagavad-gita.

> TRANSLATION: Those who worship the demigods will take birth among the demigods; those who worship ghosts and spirits will take birth among such beings; those who worship ancestors go to the ancestors; and those who worship Me will live with Me.

> PURPORT: If anyone has any desire to go to the moon, the sun, or any other planet, one can attain the desired destination by following specific Vedic principles recommended for that purpose. These are vividly described in the fruitive activities portion of the Vedas, technically known as darsa-paurnamasi, which recommends a specific worship of demigods situated on different heavenly planets. Similarly, one can attain the Pita planets by performing a specific yajna. Similarly, one can go to many ghostly planets and become a Yaksa, Raksa or Pisaca. Pisaca worship is called "black arts" or "black magic." There are many men who practice this black art, and they think that it is spiritualism, but such activities are completely materialistic. Similarly, a pure devotee, who worships the Supreme Personality of Godhead only, achieves the planets of Vaikuntha and Krishnaloka without a doubt. *(Prabhupada from Bhagavad-gita 9.25)*

Therefore by controlling the earth planet and the activities that are performed there one is able to influence the future of the souls incarnating on the planet. The demons due to their envy of the Lord always desire to exploit the earth for their own sense gratification and wish to keep people in total ignorance of the spiritual goal of human life.

The demons do not want people awakening spiritually and making progress on the path back to their original home in the spiritual world. They want a life of total forgetfulness of the Supreme Lord and they want to influence all others to such a demoniac state of existence. They even have their own planets in the lower planetary system in which they live very opulent lives but without any consciousness of the Lord.

> Below Rahu by another 1,000,000 yojanas are the planets of the Siddhas, Caranas and Vidyadharas, and below these are planets such as Yaksaloka and Raksaloka. Below these planets is the earth, and 70,000 yojanas below the earth are the lower planetary systems--Atala, Vitala, Sutala, Talatala, Mahatala, Rasatala and Patala. Demons and Raksasas live in these lower planetary systems with their wives and children, always engaged in sense gratification and not fearing their next births. The sunshine does not reach these planets, but they are illuminated by jewels fixed upon the hoods of snakes. Because of these shining gems there is practically no darkness. Those living in these planets do not become old or diseased, and they are not afraid of death from any cause but the time factor, the Supreme Personality of Godhead. *(Srimad Bhagavatam 5th Canto Intro)*

> In these seven planetary systems, which are also known as the subterranean heavens [bila-svarga], there are very beautiful houses, gardens and places of sense enjoyment, which are even more opulent than those in the higher planets because the demons have a very high standard of sensual pleasure, wealth and influence. Most of the residents of these planets, who are known as Daityas, Danavas and Nagas, live as householders. Their wives, children, friends and society are all fully engaged in illusory, material happiness. The sense enjoyment of the demigods is sometimes disturbed, but the residents of these planets enjoy life without disturbances. Thus they are understood to be very attached to illusory happiness. *(Srimad Bhagavatam 5.24.8)*

It has become very well known in the conspiracy circles that there are shape shifting reptilians trying to take over the earth planet. These beings are described in Srimad Bhagavatam and also reside in the lower planetary system. They often fight with the demigods like Indra.

TRANSLATION: The planetary system below Talatala is known as Mahatala. It is the abode of many-hooded snakes, descendants of Kadru, who are always very angry. The great snakes who are prominent are Kuhaka, Taksaka, Kaliya and Susena. The snakes in Mahatala are always disturbed by fear of Garuda, the carrier of Lord Visnu, but although they are full of anxiety, some of them nevertheless sport with their wives, children, friends and relatives.

PURPORT: It is stated here that the snakes who live in the planetary system known as Mahatala are very powerful and have many hoods. They live with their wives and children and consider themselves very happy, although they are always full of anxiety because of Garuda, who comes there to destroy them. This is the way of material life. Even if one lives in the most abominable condition, he still thinks himself happy with his wife, children, friends and relatives.

TRANSLATION: Beneath Mahatala is the planetary system known as Rasatala, which is the abode of the demoniac sons of Diti and Danu. They are called Panis, Nivata-kavacas, Kaleyas and Hiranya-puravasis [those living in Hiranya-pura]. They are all enemies of the demigods, and they reside in holes like snakes. From birth they are extremely powerful and cruel, and although they are proud of their strength, they are always defeated by the Sudarsana cakra of the Supreme Personality of Godhead, who rules all the planetary systems. When a female messenger from Indra named Sarama chants a particular curse, the serpentine demons of Mahatala become very afraid of Indra.

PURPORT: It is said that there was a great fight between these serpentine demons and Indra, the King of heaven. When the defeated demons met the female messenger Sarama, who was chanting a mantra, they became afraid, and therefore they are living in the planet called Rasatala. *(Srimad Bhagavatam*

5.24.29-30)

It is these beings and others like them that are trying to take over our earth planet, as was described by Mother Govinda dasi.

Let me quote a part of her testimony again:

> Srila Prabhupada sometimes said that a "bear-like race of beings had come from a lower planetary system, and were attempting to take over the Earth planet." This bear-like race of asuras had established themselves in Russia. And by promoting communism, a form of atheism, they were determined to convert the world to Godlessness.

Therefore if the Jews who are actually from the lower planets, and are promoting communism with the aim to convert the world to Godlessness, were fought against and nearly defeated by Adolf Hitler, doesn't this clearly prove that Hitler was an empowered Deva? Could an ordinary man have raised Germany from the depths of despair and fought so powerfully against demons from the lower planets, hell bent on taking over the world?

RABBI TEACHES THAT JEWS ARE ALIENS FROM ANOTHER PLANET HERE TO CONQUER THE EARTH

The following is from a video by Jeanice Barcelo, M.A. Educator, Researcher, and Activist.

> "Listen closely as an Israeli rabbi tells his audience that "jews" are not from this planet and are here to conquer the Earth. The teachings of this rabbi would seem to indicate that the jews are an alien race (he comes right out and says this) created for the express purpose of destroying the real Creator's order and imposing onto the Earth the order of their luciferian god.

> Here is an excerpt from this must watch video that will help us all understand the nature of what we are up against.

> Rav Michael Laitman: In fact, we are not coming from here. We came from there (points to outer space). This is Israel at their root. So we went through such a route that took us inside by, what is called the "shattering of the vessels"… the

shattering of the collective soul…

Question from the audience: Who is the chief of staff that sent the commanding unit?

Rav Michael Laitman: Him. The Creator. Israel is a part of Him…

Question from the audience: So, this chief of staff sent this commanding unit?

Rav Michael Laitman: Sent the commanding unit. Gave them strength. Gave them the connections. Everything….

But… they have no choice. He broke them. He shattered them. What does it mean? In order to put them inside the hostile land, he had to give them the same form as that hostile land. It's like we go into a country as an undercover team. And each one of us is exactly like the people of the land. Say we're being sent somewhere now – Africa for instance. So we'll take on the same shape and form of the people in Africa. The characteristics, traits, approach, interests, everything. The same exact for – inside and out… You know, it's like an undercover agent. He is there for a while, no one touches him, he has to start working, build a house, family… Everything is fine for years and years. After that, he starts doing something. He gets a reminder from outside. You gotta start working. He already forgot about it and all of a sudden they call him. Here is your commander, and this and that, you know – like in the movies… This is what's happening with us. We have to wake up. We have to remember that we have a special mission. **And really, this isn't our place. We're coming from a completely different place.** So we have to find our friends according to this awakening. Did you get a phone call? I got a phone call, he got a phone call and so on. And then we gather as a group. **So from this entire planet, we are aliens coming from a different galaxy. We receive this ray of light – this awakening – individually. And now we're gathering as groups starting to**

prep ourselves to conquer Earth. That's the mission.

Question from the audience: How do we conquer it?

Rav Michael Laitman: How do we conquer it? We're also sent the method. We're being shown everything gradually. We're being taught. Not being taught, but kind of trained and activated… which sets our minds in motion. **But in fact, it's coming from our original planet. And thanks to that original natural force we have, we will takeover those living on Earth.**

Why are you looking at me like that? You don't believe me? I'm telling you seriously! It's even more than that. **It's not a different galaxy – it's a different universe. It's a different dimension altogether. That's who we are…**

Question from the Audience: "…Why are they aliens?"

Rev. Michael Laitman: "They're aliens because…. I'm not talking about their external form – their body or their flesh and blood organs. **I'm talking about that interior that does not exist in other people in the world on Earth but only in them. It's the inner software that is in them here coming from the other world.**"

"…What we're talking about now is the phase where those undercover agents have to connect together and organize themselves **in order to conquer Earth**…"

"Whether you change humanity or join humanity -- it doesn't matter. It's the same thing - whether you say it like this or like that -- it's the same thing exactly. Because basically you are letting the light work. It's neither this group or that group do anything. It's just actions making them more sensitive for the influence of the light..."

THAT IS, LUCFER'S LIGHT! THE FALSE LIGHT. THE LIGHT THAT IS DESIGNED TO KILL ALL GOD'S

CREATIONS."

This is the light from the hoods of the snakes in the lower planetary systems.

> The sunshine does not reach these planets, but they are illuminated by jewels fixed upon the hoods of snakes. Because of these shining gems there is practically no darkness. (Srimad Bhagavatam 5th Canto Intro)

So I have proved conclusively that Adolf Hitler was a saktyavesa-avatara specifically empowered to cut down the Jewish communists, who are Raksasas and demons from the lower planetary systems trying to take over the earth.

HITLER FORETOLD IN THE BHAVIṢYA PURĀṆA

The following was posted in the comments on my video blog:

> Hitler wasn't a demigod. He was an empowered incarnation of the Lord. "After many barbarians in the guise of kings have ruled over the Earth during the Age of Kali, a saintly king named Kalmalīka will take birth among the Hūṇa people to lead a rebellion against the Daityas and their pāṣaṇḍī (atheist) stooges. After having subdued many minute kings, he will declare himself the emperor and his kingdom will stretch to the length of 40,000 yojanas. Although, inevitably, he will be defeated and his kingdom destroyed, his actions will have paved the way for the Lord's Golden Age to verily set in." (Bhaviṣya Purāṇa, Pratisarga-parva 23.63-66)

> Kalmalīka (कल्मलीक) means brightness, lustre. and the name Adolf is a compound derived from the Old High German Athalwolf, a composition of athal, or adal, meaning "noble", and wolf. The name is cognate to the Anglo-Saxon name Æthelwulf (also Eadulf or Eadwulf). The name can also be derived from the ancient Germanic elements "Wald" meaning "power", "brightness" and wolf. 40,000 yojanas roughly correspond to the Third Reich at its greatest extent.

What did Prabhupada say about the Bhaviṣya Purāṇa?

> Tamala Krishna: He says he read a passage of the Bhavisya Maha-Purana written by Vyasadeva three thousand years before Christ foretelling Jesus Christ's presence in the Himalayas in 78

of the Christian era, and his meeting with King Shalamoyi.(?) Are there any other prophecies in the Bhavisya Maha-Purana or in any other scriptures telling more accurately Jesus Christ's birthday?

Prabhupada: **Everything is accurate there.**

[Room Conversation, April 2, 1977, Bombay]

CHAPTER FOUR

Prabhupada's Jaladuta Diary

THE JOURNEY - THE JALADUTA SETS SAIL FOR AMERICA

AUGUST 1965

12 TUESDAY

To start for U.S.A. by

MV. Jaladuta from Calcutta

port (K. George's Dockyard)

13 FRIDAY

Today at 9 a.m. embarked on M.V. Jaladuta. Came with me Bhagwati, the Dwarwan of Scindia Sansir(?) Mr. Sen Gupta, Mr. Ali and Vrindaban. The cabinet is quite comfortable. It is owner's residence and therefore the sitting room, the bedroom and the bath and privy all equipped with first class materials. Everything is nice in the 1st class compartment and thanks to Lord Sri Krishna for His enlightening Smti. Sumati Moraji for all these arrangements. I am quite comfortable.

The ship started at 1/30 p.m. very slowly from the dock (and) reached near Botanical Garden and stopped at mid-stream of the Ganges till 11 p.m. and then turned towards the front and started. It is quite steady. I cannot understand in my cabin if it is at all moving. I am so comfortable. The voyage was again stopped at 3/30 a.m. at Kalpi(?) near Diamond Harbor & Ganokhali(?) wideth(?) and detained for about 8 hours. The delta of the Ganges quite wide with shallow water.

SATURDAY 14

The ship started at about 11 o'clock in the morning majestically. I do not feel any jerking whatsoever. But on reaching the Bay of Bengal, there is tilting of the ship and little rolling also. The roughness increased gradually on the upper Bay of Bengal and I felt sea sickness. There was vomiting tendency and dizziness and I felt uncomfortable the whole day and night. The sea was foamy all through. It appeared like a big plate of water extending to 40 square miles

81

but factually it was endless so, today. It is a vivid example of God's Maya because it appears like something but factually it is something else.

SUNDAY 15

In the morning I woke up and felt a little better but I felt no hunger. Took only a glass of lemon sikanjie [lemon drink/nimbu pani] but the head dizziness is continuing. Up to 10/30 I was in the captain's room, radio room, chatting with the officers. In the radio room they were despatching news to other ships. The captain's room is full with nautical paraphernalia. I saw a chart of different appearancial(?) photo of the sea. The grades are 0 to 10 degrees and I think we are passing on the sea between 4 to 7 points the scene of the 10th point was furious and the 12th serious. The captain advised me to take more solid food.

MONDAY 16

Today early in the morning I saw that the ship is plying on the surface of the sea almost on 0 degree of waves. Yesterday night was comfortable and although I did not take my lunch, I took a little chara-murki [puffed rice/chidwa] with milk. The ship ran all the night yesterday smoothly and the sky although not very clear there was moon light in the night. In the morning there was sunshine but after 11 the sea became a little more rough showing foamy waves from distance. After passing the latitude of Trichinopoli we experienced a dark cloud subsequently raining all over the sea. The siren sounded on account (of) hazy vision to warn other ships coming from opposite direction. At about 12 noon it is raining heavily and the ship is stopped moving occasionally sounding the siren. There is constant sounds of thunderbolt. This is the first time I am experiencing heavy rains in the midst of deep ocean. From 12 noon we are passing through cyclonic weather. The ship is tilting too much. I felt sea sickness all day and night. At 3 p.m. the ship turned towards Ceylon coast and we are now in the Ceylon water.

17 TUESDAY

Today morning the sky is scattered with cloud. The ship is going toward western side. I feel a little bit well after passing my stool. The ship is running against wind current. The sea is little rougher. At 10/30 we saw the south coast of Ceylon with a white light house. Two ships passed from the opposite side. Some daring fishermen were fishing in small boats. From distance they appeared to be almost drowned in the water but next moment they appear to be safely working. There is sunshine but the sky is not clear. The captain informed me that by next six hours we shall reach Colombo port. The hilly southernmost Ceylon coast is said to be 4 to 5 miles away from our ship. This means the fishermen were fishing in small boats 5 to 10 miles away from their native coast. Certainly very daring job. At about 2 p.m. we have now turned towards northern front. The sky is cloudy but we are forwarding steadily. Today I was better than other three days. At 3 p.m. the Colombo city became faintly visible from the ship. The colour of water in the India ocean is different from that of Bay of Bengal. The ship reached exactly at 4/30 in the port but the management of Colombo port could not receive the ship for want of berth and then it is anchored on the shore waiting to enter the port. At about 9 p.m. the ship was escorted by the Pilot and we entered the dockyard very old pattern(?) but there were many ships from various countries including passenger and cargo ships. At night the dockyard ships assumed a brilliant (sic:) espectacle on account profuse light. We rested the whole night the ship being anchored. Next morning barges loaded with goods arrived near the ship.

18 WEDNESDAY

Today 18/8/65 I felt quite normal and the sea-sickness completely removed. The ship remained silent the whole day on account of hazy sky and only a few loads of goods were admitted. I wanted to see the Colombo city but I could not make any arrangement. The ship was standing at the midstream and I did not like to go alone.

19 THURSDAY

The next morning 19/8/65 I informed my situation to Captain Pandia and he was very kind to take me to the shore in a motor launch. We dropped at Elizabeth gate talked with some Ceylonese clerks and then in a taxi we went to the office of Narottam & Pierera Co. The manager Mr. Banka was a Gujarati gentleman and he received us well. He arranged for me a good car to go round the city. The office quarter was quite busy and many foreign offices and renowned Banks were there. I saw the Governor General's House, the Parliament House, the Town Hall (and) one very nice sea-side Hotel and passed through very nice clean roads, bazars. The city appeared to be nice and clean and the small bungalows nicely decorated. It appears that people although not very good looking they are not uncultured neither they are tasteless. The city is quite up to resembling an Indian city like Madras and Poona(?) The buses and taxis were clean to see. The bus stands almost crowded like that of the Indian cities. The offices conducted almost in Indian style. The culture and civilization is Indian cent per cent but artificially India and Ceylon is divided. We starting for Cochin at 6 p.m. The ship started at 7 p.m., the pilot being late in reaching the ship. It ran for the whole night and next day up to 3/30 p.m. and reached the coast of Cochin. The ship is standing on the coast of Cochin without entering the dock.

FRIDAY 20

Today at (20/8/65) the captain arranged for a meeting on board the M/V

Jaladuta on account of Janmastami day and I spoke for an hour on the philosophy and teachings of Lord Sri Krishna. All the officers attended the meeting and there was distribution of Prasadam. The matter was radiographed to Smt. Sumati Moraji in Bombay. The ship is stranded on the Arabian Sea about 4 miles away from the coast. We are in this position from 3/20 p.m. 20/8/65 to 9/30 a.m. on 22/8/65.

SUNDAY 22

At about 10 a.m. we are now in the dockyard of Cochin. The dock is peculiar because it is by nature full of small islands. Some of the islands are full with nice hutments formerly known as British Island. I saw my books from Bombay arrived in five cases and the agents loaded them on the ship at 4 p.m. on 22/8/65. The agent m/s Jairam & Sons kindly sent their car for my driving in the city. Out of the group of islands two big islands joined by an iron over-bridge are known as Cochin and Ernakulam. The iron over bridge was constructed by the Britishers very nicely along with railway lines. The railways line is extended up to the Port. There are many flourishing foreign firms and banks. It is (?) Sunday, the bazar was closed. I saw a peculiar kind of plantain available in this part of the country. The island known as Coachin is not an up to date city. The roads are like narrow lanes. The part of the city where the foreigners are residing are well situated. The buildings factories, etc. all big and(?) well maintained. The mohamedan quarters are separate from the Hindu quarters as usual in other Indian cities. The part known as Ernakulam is up to date. There is a nice park on the bank of the gulf and it is named Subhas Bose Park. It is good that Subhas Babu is popular in this part of the country. I saw the Kerala High Court and the public buildings, the High Court being situated in Ernakulam it appears that the city is capital of Kerala. This Official Bhadra 31 days 1887 Saka part of India resembles Bengal scenario and the city Ernakulum also Cochin appears to me like old Kalighat or Tollygunge area of Calcutta. The culture is Indian as usual.

Official Bhadra 31 days 18887 Saka

23 MONDAY

Today Annada Ekadashi

We started towards Red sea on the western front at about 12/30 noon. The sky was almost clear and there was sunshine since the starting of the trip from

Cochin port. We are floating now on the Arabian sea. My sea sickness again began. Headache vomiting tendency no hunger dizziness and no energy to work. It is continuing. There are sometimes showers of rain but for a short time. There was a fellow passenger in my cabin. He is also attacked with sea sickness. The whole night passed

24 TUESDAY

Today at about 1/30 p.m. I enquired from wheel-room that we have come only 400 miles off the Indian coast. My sea-sickness is still continuing. I take my meals once only but today I could not take my full meals also although I was fasting yesterday. I (am) feeling uncomfortable.

25 WEDNESDAY

Beginning from today down

26 THURSDAY

27 FRIDAY

28 SATURDAY

29 SUNDAY

30 MONDAY

31 TUESDAY

Passed over a great crisis on the struggle for life and death.

A separate statement has to be written on this crisis area.

SEPTEMBER 1965

1 WEDNESDAY

Port Suez

2 THURSDAY

Suez Canal & Port Said

3 FRIDAY

We started from Port Said today at about 1 p.m. The Port Said city is nice. It has long narrow neat and clean roads with lofty buildings. The city is not at all congested. While passing the rear point of Suez towards Mediterranean sea, the city is clearly seen. But it is a small city with some industrial factories. Although in the desert in the city all varieties of vegetables available. There is also a Marine drive like Bombay Chowpatty beach. I could see a good park in the city.

4 SATURDAY

There was a rehearsal for emergency. We all prepared with belt on the body and the life boat was tested whether they were in order. There were two boats with capacity to load 120 persons. But we were all about fifty five on the board.

5 SUNDAY

In the evening the sky was cloudy and they expected foggy weather and all of them became little gloomy. But at midnight we passed Malta Sicily by God's grace it was all right throughout the night.

6 MONDAY

Today I have taken khichri and kari. It was tasteful. and I took them with relish and this gave me a push forward to get renewed strength little by little.

TUESDAY 7

Today Baraha Dwadashi observed

The best atmospheric condition on the Mediterranean sea. All along we have seen the Algerian coast.

WEDNESDAY 8

Today at about 8 o'clock in the morning and near about Gibraltar we had a first experience of fog impediment. It was all dark round the ship and she stopped moving completely She was whistling now and then to protect herself from other unseen ships being collided with. We started at about 11 again.

8/9/65 at about 2/30 p.m. we passed over Gibraltar Port ending at Tarita(?) Light House. The other side is Spanish Morocco There is regular ferry steamer service. The srt.(?) is wide about seven miles across. We are in the Atlantic.

THURSDAY 9

Till 4 o'clock afternoon we have crossed over the Atlantic Ocean for twenty four hours. The whole day was clear and almost smooth. I am taking my food regularly and got some strength to struggle. There is slight lurching(?) of the ship and I am feeling slight headache also. But I am struggling and the nectarine of life is Sri Chaitanya Charitamrita the source of my all vitality.

10 FRIDAY

Today the ship is plying very smoothly. I feel today better. But I am feeling separation from Sri Vrindaban and my Lords Sri Govinda, Gopinath, Radha Damodar. The only solace is Sri Chaitanya Charitamrita in which I am tasting the nectarine of Lord Chaitanya's Leela. I have left Bharat Bhumi just to execute the order of Sri Bhakti Siddhanta Saraswati in pursuance of Lord Chaitanya's order. I have no qualification, but I have taken up the risk just to carry out the order of His Divine Grace. I depend fully on Their mercy so far away from Vrindaban.

11 SATURDAY

Today the ship ran on very smoothly. The sky was clear and there was sunshine all the day. At about 7/30 in the morning we passed on the Azore group islands under the Portugal Republic. There was again rehearsal for life boat saving at 4/30 p.m. There was rehearsal of the fire brigadiers also. At night there was profuse moonlight on the ocean and considerable lurching also. But did not affect me very much as it used to do in the Arabian sea. The Atlantic Ocean is more kind to me than all other seas so far we have crossed over. It is all Lord Krishna's Grace.

12 SUNDAY

S. R. Day. Today there is a great deal of lurching although the sky is clear. Mrs. Pandiya although a little lady but very intelligent and learned also. She has foretold about my future. Thanks to her prediction. All blessings of Lord Krishna for her. The crisis which I suppose to have crossed is also mentioned by her. If I have crossed the crisis, then that is Good Will of Lord Krishna my friend and philosopher. In the evening there was too much lurching and I felt a bit sea-sickness. I could not take my food properly. A little sweets were accepted with some relish. The lurching continued till midnight.

MONDAY 13

Today is the 32nd day of our journey from Calcutta. After midnight yesterday the lurching decreased and I felt relief. In the morning also I could not take my breakfast properly. Then I cooked 'Bati-chachari(?).' It appeared to be delicious and I was able to take some food. Today I have disclosed my mind to my companion Lord Sri Krishna. There is a Bengali poem made by me today in this connection. At about eleven there is a little lurching. The captain tells that they had never such calmness of the Atlantic. I said it is Lord Krishna's mercy. His wife asked me to come back again with them so that they may have again a calm Atlantic Ocean. If Atlantic would have shown its usual face perhaps I would have died. But Lord Krishna has taken charge of the ship.

TUESDAY 14

Today is the 33rd day of our journey and at 3 o'clock in the morning I saw the sky cloudy with dim moon-light. From morning till 1 o'clock the sky remained cloudy and at 1/30 p.m. there was a shower of rain. The sky is still cloudy and the wind is blowing from south-east corner and raining at intervals. The whole day passed in that way and the wind assumed a para-cyclonic face with dense cloud resulting in rain till 9/30 p.m. with regular lightening etc. At ten o'clock when I was talking in the captain's room the chief engineer Mr. Travers told me that he had never such experience of calm & quietness of the Atlantic Ocean. There was always typhoon, cyclone, fog, etc. at least for days in every trip in the past(?). I said it is Lord Krishna's Grace. If such things as usual in Atlantic would have taken place, I would die.

WEDNESDAY 15

Today 34th day of our journey As usual I rise up at 3 a.m. and when I went to veranda I saw the sky almost clear. There was moon-shine on head(?) and although the wind from south-east was strong, the ocean was clear visioned and the ship was passing smoothly. At about 11 a.m. the sky again became over cast with cloud and it is continued till 3 p.m. There was rainfalls at intervals but after 4 o'clock the sky became clear and there was bright sunshine. I was engaged in reading Kaliya Daman Leela from Srimad Bhagwatam specially the prayers by Srimati Naga Patnis and the last appealing prayer by Kaliya.

AMERICA - SRILA PRABHUPADA ARRIVES AT BOSTON HARBOR

THURSDAY 16

Today is the 35th day of our journey and yesterday night at about 10/30 p.m. we have turned one wheel(?) towards north eastern corner from the Bermuda latitude towards Boston port. In the morning the atmosphere was fairly cleared and the ship was plying very smoothly. The first officer told me that they never had such experience of the Atlantic ocean and he ascribed the good luck to me. I said yes it is all Lord Krishna's Grace because due to my severe type of sea-sickness, He has Himself taken charge of the ship. In (?) expansion the Lord is rowing the oars. We shall certainly reach to America port safely. The whole day was clear sun-shine but at 4 p.m. the sky all of a sudden became foggy. The sun became dim covered by foggy weather. The horizon is still visible. Let us see what is still ahead. The ship is stopped completely at about 6 p.m. on account of dense fog. Be Lord Krishna pleased to get out this fog. By the Grace of Lord Krishna the fog was cleared after 2-3 hours and the ship started. The whole night was non-disturbing and today on the 36th day of our journey we reached safely at Boston Port at 5/30 a.m.

17 FRIDAY

We are now on the dockyard of Boston and at 10 a.m. the custom officers and others came on the ship. They have now issued the admittance permission after due checking etc. I saw the Boston Town with captain It is very nice and I shall describe it in a separate note. 36th day from starting from Calcutta Port To-day we are expected to reach Boston Port U.S.A. in the morning ACB—/9/65

We stayed the whole day & night at Boston till 4.p.m. next day

18 SATURDAY

To-day is the 37th day of our journey & at 4 p.m. we left Boston Port for New York. In the morning I had telephonic talks with Gopal P. Agarwal in Butler and he said that his man will receive me at New York & dispatch me to Butler by Bus or train as convenient. I tried to contact Dr. Misra but he was not available both yesterday and to-day. I do not know if he is coming to receive me. To-day I met two American nice gentlemen Mr. Gardiner & Fryer(?). We passed a beautiful canal and crossed underneath two overbridges. But at midnight there was considerable fog disturbance and the ship moved very slowly. The fog persisted till we reached late at New York Port at 12/30 on 19/9/65.

SUNDAY 19

Today is the 38th day of our journey and we reached New York Port at 12/30 p.m. about three hours later than the scheduled time.

SATURDAY 25

Today I have sent letter to Captain Arun Pandiya.

NOVEMBER 1965

THURSDAY 11

Paragon Book
Gallery New York
Received today 25 sets
from Gopal.
5 sets personally
10 " through Orientalia
25 "   "   Paragon
40 sets
ACB

SUNDAY 14

Meeting with Krishna K. Dhandip
No. 152 West 13th Street
New York N.Y. at 5 p.m.

SUNDAY 28

Meeting at New India House
"God Consciousness"
under the auspices of the
Tagore Society of New York.

MEMORANDA

1. The Absolute Truth

(Srimad Bhagawatam 1st Canto)

2. Symptoms of Objectivity

 (Srimad Bhagwatam 2nd Canto)

3. Creation of Material World.

 (Srimad Bhagwatam 3rd Canto)

4. The Sub-Creators.

(Srimad Bhagwatam 4th Canto)

5. The Planetary System.

(Srimad Bhagwatam 5th Canto)

6. Lord the Protector

(Srimad Bhagwatam 6th Canto)

7. Creative Impetus

(Srimad Bhagwatam 7th Canto)

8. Change of Manpower

(Srimad Bhagwatam 8th Canto)

9. The Science of God

(Srimad Bhagwatam 9th Canto)

10. Krishna The Cause of All Causes.

(Srimad Bhagwatam 10th Canto)

11. The Path of Liberation

(Srimad Bhagwatam 11th Canto)

12. The Summum Bonum.

(Srimad Bhagwatam 12th Canto)

MEMORANDA

1. The Absolute Truth
   (Srimad Bhagawatam 1st Canto)

2. Symptoms of Objectivity
   (Srimad Bhagwatam 2nd Canto)

3. Creation of Material World.
   (Srimad Bhagwatam 3rd Canto)

4. The Sub-Creators.
   (Srimad Bhagwatam 4th Canto)

5. The Planetary System.
   (Srimad Bhagwatam 5th Canto)

6. Lord the Protector
   (Srimad Bhagwatam 6th Canto)

7. The Creative Impetus
   (Srimad Bhagwatam 7th Canto)

8. Change of Manpower
   (Srimad Bhagwatam 8th Canto)

9. The Science of God
   (Srimad Bhagwatam 9th Canto)

10. Krishna The Cause of All Causes.
    (Srimad Bhagwatam 10th Canto)

11. The Path of Liberation
    (Srimad Bhagwatam 11th Canto)

12. The Summum Bonum.
    (Srimad Bhagwatam 12th Canto)

SCINDIA'S CARGO SERVICE SPANS FOUR CONTINENTS

CHAPTER FIVE

Prayers Written by Srila Prabhupada Aboard the Jaladuta

Prayer to the Lotus Feet of Kṛṣṇa

By His Divine Grace A.C. Bhaktivedanta Swami Prabhupāda

On board the ship Jaladuta, September 13, 1965

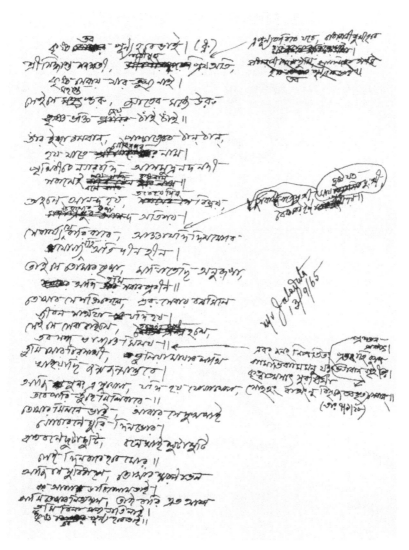

(refrain)

krsna taba punya habe bhāi
e-punya koribe jabe rādhārāṇī khuśī habe
dhruva ati bali tomā tāi

I emphatically say to you, O brothers, you will obtain your
good fortune from the Supreme Lord Kṛṣṇa only when
Śrīmatī Rādhārāṇī becomes pleased with you.

śrī-siddhānta saraswatī śacī-suta priya ati
krsna-sebāya jāra tula nāi
sei se mohānta-guru jagater madhe uru
krsna-bhakti dey thāi thāi

Śrī Śrīmad Bhaktisiddhānta Sarasvatī Ṭhākura, who is very dear to
Lord Gaurāṅga, the son of Mother Śacī, is unparalleled in his service to
the Supreme Lord Śrī Kṛṣṇa. He is that great saintly spiritual master who
bestows intense devotion to Kṛṣṇa at different places throughout the world.

tāra icchā balavān pāścātyete thān thān
hoy jāte gaurāṅger nām
prthivīte nagarādi āsamudra nada nadī
sakalei loy krsna nām

By his strong desire, the holy name of Lord Gaurāṅga will spread
throughout all the countries of the Western world. In all the cities,
towns, and villages on the earth, from all the oceans, seas, rivers,
and streams, everyone will chant the holy name of Kṛṣṇa.

tāhale ānanda hoy tabe hoy digvijay
caitanyer krpā atiśay
māyā dusta jata duhkhī jagate sabāi sukhī
vaisnaver icchā pūrna hoy

As the vast mercy of Śrī Caitanya Mahāprabhu conquers
all directions, a flood of transcendental ecstasy will certainly
cover the land. When all the sinful, miserable living entities
become happy, the Vaiṣṇavas' desire is then fulfilled.

se kārja je koribāre ājñā jadi dilo more
jogya nahi an dīna hīna
tāi se tomāra krpā māgitechi anurūpā

āji tumi sabār pravīṇa

Although my Guru Mahārāja ordered me to accomplish this mission,
I am not worthy or fit to do it. I am very fallen and insignificant.
Therefore, O Lord, now I am begging for Your mercy so that I may
become worthy, for You are the wisest and most experienced of all.

tomāra se śakti pele guru-sebāya bastu mile
jībana sārthak jadi hoy
sei se sevā pāile tāhale sukhī hale
taba saṅga bhāgyate miloy

If You bestow Your power, by serving the spiritual master
one attains the Absolute Truth-one's life becomes successful.
If that service is obtained, then one becomes happy and
gets Your association due to good fortune.

evaṁ janaṁ nipatitaṁ prabhavāhikūpe
kāmābhikāmam anu yaḥ prapatan prasaṅgāt
kṛtvātmasāt surarṣiṇā bhagavan gṛhītaḥ
so 'haṁ kathaṁ nu visṛje tava bhṛtya-sevām

My dear Lord, O Supreme Personality of Godhead, because of my
association with material desires, one after another, I was gradually
falling into a blind well full of snakes, following the general populace.
But Your servant Nārada Muni kindly accepted me as his disciple and
instructed me how to achieve this transcendental position. Therefore,
my first duty is to serve him. How could I leave his service?
(Prahlāda Mahārāja to Lord Nṛsiṁhadeva, Bhāg. 7.9.28)

tumi mor cira sāthī bhuliyā māyār lāthi
khāiyāchi janma-janmāntare
āji punaḥ e sujoga jadi hoy jogāyoga
tabe pāri tuhe milibāre

O Lord Kṛṣṇa, You are my eternal companion. Forgetting You,
I have suffered the kicks of māyā birth after birth. If today the chance
to meet You occurs again, then I will surely be able to rejoin You.

tomāra milane bhāi ābār se sukha pāi
gocārane ghuri din bhor
kata bane chuṭāchuṭi bane khāi luṭāpuṭi
sei din kabe habe mor

O dear friend, in Your company I will experience great joy once again. In the early morning I will wander about the cowherd pastures and fields. Running and frolicking in the many forests of Vraja, I will roll on the ground in spiritual ecstasy. Oh when will that day be mine?

āji se subidhāne tomāra smaraṇa bhela
baro āśā ḍākilām tāi
āmi tomāra nitya-dāsa tāi kori eta āśa
tumi binā anya gati nāi

Today that remembrance of You came to me in a very nice way. Because I have a great longing I called to You. I am Your eternal servant and therefore I desire Your association so much. O Lord Kṛṣṇa, except for You there is no other means of success.

Mārkine Bhāgavata-dharma

By His Divine Grace A.C. Bhaktivedanta Swami Prabhupāda

At Boston Harbor, September 18, 1965

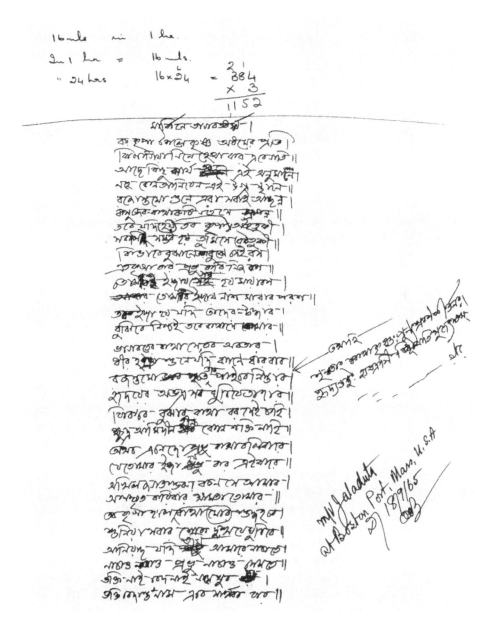

baro-kṛpā kaile kṛṣṇa adhamer prati
ki lāgiyānile hethā koro ebe gati

My dear Lord Kṛṣṇa, You are so kind upon this useless
soul, but I do not know why You have brought me here.
Now You can do whatever You like with me.

āche kichu kārja taba ei anumāne
nahe keno āniben ei ugra-sthāne

But I guess You have some business here, otherwise
why would You bring me to this terrible place?

rajas tamo guṇe erā sabāi ācchanna
bāsudeb-kathā ruci nahe se prasanna

Most of the population here is covered by the material modes
of ignorance and passion. Absorbed in material life, they think
themselves very happy and satisfied, and therefore they have no
taste for the transcendental message of Vāsudeva. I do not
know how they will be able to understand it.

tabe jadi taba kṛpā hoy ahaitukī
sakal-i sambhava hoy tumi se kautukī

But I know Your causeless mercy can make everything
possible because You are the most expert mystic.

ki bhāve bujhāle tārā bujhe sei rasa
eta kṛpā koro prabhu kori nija-baśa

How will they understand the mellows of devotional service?
O Lord, I am simply praying for Your mercy so that I will
be able to convince them about Your message.

tomāra icchāya saba hoy māyā-baśa
tomāra icchāya nāśa māyār paraśa

All living entities have come under the control of the illusory
energy by Your will, and therefore, if You like, by Your will
they can also be released from the clutches of illusion.

taba icchā hoy jadi tādera uddhār
bujhibe niścai tabe kathā se tomār

I wish that You may deliver them. Therefore if You so desire their
deliverance, then only will they be able to understand Your message.

bhāgavater kathā se taba avatar
dhīra haiyā śune jadi kāne bār bār

The words of Śrīmad-Bhāgavatam are Your incarnation, and
if a sober person repeatedly receives it with submissive aural
reception, then he will be able to understand Your message.

It is said in the Śrīmad-Bhāgavatam (1.2.17-21):

śrnvatāṁ sva-kathāḥ kṛṣṇaḥ
punya-śravaṇa-kīrtanaḥ
hṛdy antaḥ-stho hy abhadrāṇi
vidhunoti suhṛt satām

naṣṭa-prāyeṣv abhadreṣu
nityaṁ bhāgavata-sevayā
bhagavaty uttama-śloke
bhaktir bhavati naiṣṭhikī

tadā rajas-tamo-bhāvāḥ
kāma-lobhādayaś ca ye
ceta etair anāviddhaṁ
sthitaṁ sattve prasīdati

evaṁ prasanna-manaso
bhagavad-bhakti-yogataḥ
bhagavat-tattva-vijñānaṁ
mukta-saṅgasya jāyate

bhidyate hṛdaya-granthiś
chidyante sarva-saṁśayāḥ
kṣīyante cāsya karmāṇi
dṛṣṭa evātmanīśvare

"Śrī Kṛṣṇa, the Personality of Godhead, who is the Paramātmā [Supersoul]
in everyone's heart and the benefactor of the truthful devotee, cleanses
desire for material enjoyment from the heart of the devotee who has

developed the urge to hear His messages, which are in
themselves virtuous when properly heard and chanted.

By regular attendance in classes on the Bhāgavatam and by rendering
of service to the pure devotee, all that is troublesome to the heart is
almost completely destroyed, and loving service unto the Personality
of Godhead, who is praised with transcendental songs,
is established as an irrevocable fact.

As soon as irrevocable loving service is established in the heart,
the effects of nature's modes of passion and ignorance, such as lust,
desire and hankering, disappear from the heart. Then the devotee
is established in goodness, and he becomes completely happy.

Thus established in the mode of unalloyed goodness, the man whose
mind has been enlivened by contact with devotional service to the Lord
gains positive scientific knowledge of the Personality of Godhead
in the stage of liberation from all material association.

Thus the knot in the heart is pierced, and all misgivings are cut to pieces.
The chain of fruitive actions is terminated when one sees the self as master."

rajas tamo hate tabe pāibe nistār
hṛdayer abhadra sate ghucibe tāhār

He will become liberated from the influence of the modes of
ignorance and passion and thus all inauspicious things
accumulated in the core of the heart will disappear.

ki ko're bujhābo kathā baro sei cāhi
khudra āmi dīna hīna kono śakti nāhi

How will I make them understand this message of Kṛṣṇa
consciousness? I am very unfortunate, unqualified and the most
fallen. Therefore I am seeking Your benediction so that I can
convince them, for I am powerless to do so on my own.

athaca enecho prabhu kathā bolibāre
je tomār icchā prabhu koro ei bāre

Somehow or other, O Lord, You have brought me here to speak about You.
Now, my Lord, it is up to You to make me a success or failure as You like.

akhila jagat-guru! bacana se āmār
alaṅkṛta koribār khamatā tomār

O spiritual master of all the worlds! I can simply repeat
Your message, so if You like You can make my power
of speaking suitable for their understanding.

taba kṛpā ha'le mor kathā śuddha habe
śuniyā sabāra śoka duḥkha je ghucibe

Only by Your causeless mercy will my words become pure.
I am sure that when this transcendental message penetrates
their hearts they will certainly feel engladdened and thus
become liberated from all unhappy conditions of life.

āniyācho jadi prabhu āmāre nācāte
nācāo nācāo prabhu nācāo se-mate
kāṣṭhera puttali jathā nācāo se-mate

O Lord, I am just like a puppet in Your hands. So if You have
brought me here to dance, then make me dance, make
me dance, O Lord, make me dance as You like.

bhakti nāi beda nāi nāme khub daro
"bhaktivedānta" nām ebe sārthak kor

I have no devotion, nor do I have any knowledge,
but I have strong faith in the holy name of Kṛṣṇa. I have
been designated as Bhaktivedānta, and now, if You like,
You can fulfill the real purport of Bhaktivedānta.

Signed-the most unfortunate, insignificant beggar

A.C. Bhaktivedanta Swami,

on board the ship Jaladuta, Commonwealth Pier,
Boston, Massachusetts, U.S.A. Dated 18th of September, 1965

CHAPTER SIX

India's Message Of Peace And Goodwill

"SRIMAD BHAGWATAM"

INDIA'S MESSAGE OF
PEACE AND GOODWILL

Sixty Volumes of Elaborate English Version by

Tridandi Goswami
A. C. BHAKTIVEDANTA SWAMI.

CARRIED BY
THE SCINDIA STEAM NAV. CO., LIMITED
BOMBAY.

All over the world for scientific knowledge of God.

Srila Prabhupada's pamphlet for the spreading of Lord Krishna's teachings

"SRIMAD BHAGWATAM"

INDIA'S MESSAGE OF PEACE AND GOODWILL

Sixty Volumes of Elaborate English Version by

Tridandi Goswami

A.C. BHAKTIVEDANTA SWAMI

CARRIED BY

THE SCINDIA STEAM NAV. CO., LIMITED

BOMBAY

All over the world for scientific knowledge of God.

The sufferings of the entire human society can at once be brought under control simply by individual practice of "Bhaktiyoga" a simple and easy process of chanting the holy Name of God. Every country, every nation and every community throughout the world has some conception of the holy Name of God and as such either the Hindus or the Mohammedans or the Christians every one can easily chant the holy Name of God in a meditative mood and that will bring about the required peace and good will in the present problematic human society.

Any enquiry in this connection will be gladly answered by Sri Swamiji.

The Hindus generally chant the holy Name of God in sixteen chain of transcendental sound composed of 32 alphabets as "Hare krishna, hare krishna, krishna krishna hare hare., Hare rama, hare rama, rama rama, hare hare." The Vedic literatures like the Upanisads and the Puranas do recommend chanting of the abovementioned sixteen holy Names at a stretch and Lord Sri Chaitanya, Who preached this cult of chanting the holy Name of God, gave special importance on these transcendental sounds. In this Age of Kali or the age of hate, hypocrisy, corruption and quarrel, the only remedial measure is that every man should chant the holy Name of the Lord both individually and collectively.

The Glories of the holy Name have been described by Sri Chaitanya in His eight verses of "Siksastak" which run as follows:—

1. Glory to the Sri Krishna Samkirtanam which cleanses the heart of all the dust accumulated for years together and thus the fire of conditional life of repeated birth and death is extinguished. Such Samkirtan movement is the prime benediction for the humanity at large because it spreads rays of the benediction - Moon. It is the life of transcendental knowledge, it increases the ocean of transcendental bliss and it helps to have a taste of the full nectarine for which always anxious we are.

2. Oh my Lord! Your holy Name can alone render all benediction upon the living being and therefore you have hundreds and millions of Names like

Krishna, Govinda etc. In these transcendental Names you have invested all your transcendental potencies and there is no hard and fast rules for chanting these holy Names. Oh my Lord! You have so kindly made easy approach to you by your holy Names but unfortunate as I am, I have no attraction for them.

3. One can chant the holy Names of the Lord in an humble state of mind thinking himself as lower than the straw on the streets, tolerant more than the tree, devoid of all sense of false prestige and being ready to offer all kinds of respects to others.

4. Oh the almighty Lord, I have no desire for accumulating wealth nor I have any desire to enjoy beautiful woman; neither I want any number of followers of mine. What I want only is that I may have your causeless devotional service in my life birth after birth.

5. Oh the son of Maharaj Nanda, I am your eternal servitor and although I am so, some how or other I have fallen on the ocean of birth and death. Please therefore pick me up from the ocean of death and fix me up as one of the atoms of your lotus feet.

6. Oh my Lord when shall my eyes be decorated with tears of love flowing incessantly by chanting your holy Name? And when all the holes of hairs on my body will have erruptions by the recitation of your Name?

7. Oh Govinda, feeling your separation, I am considering a moment as 12 twelve years or more than that and tears flowing down my cheeks like the torrents of rains. I am feeling all vacant in the world without your presence.

8. I do not know any one except Krishna as my Lord and He shall remain as such even if he handles me roughly by His embrace or He may make me broken hearted by not being present before me. He is completely free to do anything but he is always my worshipful Lord, unconditionally.

Chanting of the holy Name of God is recommended for every one both for the mass of people and the class of people. Those who are scholars, philosophers, scientists, religionists and educated, may read the English version of SRIMAD BHAGWATAM by A.C. Bhaktivedanta Swami with particular attention to the purports appended with each and every verse.They have appreciated the publication as follows:—

"At a time when not only the people of India but those of the west need the chastening quality of love and truth in a corrupting atmosphere of hate and hypocrisy, a work like this will have uplifting and corrective influence. What is God? He is truth, He is love. Even an atheist must accept the supremacy of those qualities and how much they are needed by the people of the world who have been tought to deny God and these qualities, do not require much emphasis."

"The author has attempted a tremendous task... A perusal will give us in the sample measure a knowledge of the original. The essence of Srimad

Bhagwatam is the exposition of the Absolute Truth, we would recommend this book."

"The editor's vast and deep study of the subject and critical insight are reflected in these notes and."

"We have no doubt that with the publication of these volumes the rightful interpretations of the Bhagwatam, which has been the gift of Sri Chaitanya and His Goswami followers, has now been available to the English knowing world for the first time."

"The elaborate method is very helpful to the ardent student of Bhagwatam who lack in Sanskrit language. It is admitted in all hands that Bhagwatam is the most difficult text amongst the puranas. The author richly deserve the gratitude of the devotees for his pious learned labour of love."

"These volumes speak very highly of Swamiji's scholarship and specially of his love of cultural pursuits, when we look into the enormous labour and sacrifice in producing them single-handed and that too, at ripe old age of 68. We earnestly pray to the Almighty that He may spare Swamiji for all the years he may require to finish the Magnum opus of 60 volumes, and earn the love and gratitude of his fellowmen in pursuit of Divine Love and Grace, nay of the entire humanity."

"You have done a first class work and you desire the hearty commendations of every Indian every Hindu. Your deep and penetrating study of the subject and your philosophic insight are reflected in this book." etc. etc.

The Great Sinister Movement Controlling ISKCON

Srila Prabhupada said the great sinister movement entered ISKCON in 1970. There has been much discussion in regards to what this sinister movement actually is. Some say it is a group of ambitious pseudo disciples. Others say it is the envious Godbrothers from the Gaudiya Math. And still, others say it is a secret society such as the Illuminati. Let us look in more detail at this interesting topic by analyzing Prabhupada's various statements.

**It is a fact however that the great
sinister movement is within our society**

Regarding the poisonous effect in our Society, it is a fact and I know where from this poison tree has sprung up and how it affected practically the whole Society in a very dangerous form. But it does not matter. Prahlada Maharaja was administered poison, but it did not act. Similarly Lord Krishna and the Pandavas were administered poison and it did not act. I think in the same parampara system that the poison administered to our Society will not act if some of our students are as good as Prahlada Maharaja. I have therefore given the administrative power to the Governing Body Commission. (GBC) .... You are also one of the members of the GBC, so you can think over very deeply how to save the situation. **It is a fact however that the great sinister movement is within our Society**. *[Srila Prabhupada Letter to: Hamsaduta 2 September, 1970]*

Srila Prabhupada is very precise with his usage of words and he says the word "movement" which is not just one or two individuals. In fact not only does Prabhupada call it a movement but he says **"THE GREAT SINISTER MOVEMENT"**. What is the great sinister movement in this world?

If anyone does some research, he will come to the conclusion that International Jewry is the great sinister movement on this planet. They are the ones who have been working in the background manipulating world events through their control of gold and global media and who were the victors of the Second World War. It is very clear that they are the Hiranyakasipu's of these times.

These demons who have an ultimate goal to create a new world order without God, became aware of Prabhupada and his philosophy at least as early as December 26th, 1968 when Prabhupada was interviewed by an LA Times Reporter about the Moon Trip. [The Jews control all mainstream media so as to feed the people only the info they want them to hear] Thus they would have become very disturbed to hear Prabhupada exposing their planned attempts to cheat the public out of billions of tax dollars via their fake moon landing scam. They would also have become aware that if Prabhupada's basic principles of no meat eating, no intoxication, no illicit sex and no gambling was followed by the masses that would completely finish their demoniac civilization. Prabhupada talked about this point in 1976:

If they, the movement goes and becomes very strong, then our business will be lost. Kill him.

Prabhupada: So this movement should be pushed very vigorously. And so far, we have become successful. **And enemies will be always, as soon as there is something good. That is the way of material world.** Even Krishna had enemies, what to speak of us. Eh? So many enemies, but He was powerful; He killed all them. Nobody could kill Him, but there was attempt to kill Him from the very beginning of His birth. He had so many enemies. As soon as Kamsa heard that his sister is now newly married, but as soon as there was some foretelling, "Ah, you are taking care of your sister so nicely. The eighth child of this sister will kill you." "Oh, where is your child? Where is pregnancy?" Nothing. He became angry. "So why wait for eighth child? Kill my sister." Long, long before taking birth of Krishna, the mother was to be killed. This is the position of this material world. So he became so bad that "My sister..." He did not consider that "She is my sister, and she is just newly married. Where is pregnancy? Where is child? And that is the eighth child, and what will happen after that?" No consideration. Immediately, "Kill him, kill her." This is the position. **So we are instructing: no intoxication. So those who are flourishing by selling cigarettes and wine and liquor, they do not... "Immediately kill him."** Oh, yes, in this way. **"If they, the movement goes and becomes very strong, then our business will be lost. Kill him."** So naturally they will be enemies.** The same thing, the Kamsa saw that "This my sister, now she is married. So although it will take some long time, but here is the cause." **So they are thinking like that. No meat-eating, then all slaughterhouses will be closed: "They're enemy."** Although there is no such symptom that slaughterhouse is going to be closed, but they'll think like

that. They'll think like that, the same way. There is no ex... (break) ...pregnancy, first, second, third, then eighth, and the child will go, take birth and... They are thinking like that. **So the modern civilization, we are everyone saying. Because you have forbidden: no illicit sex, no intoxication, no meat-eating, no gambling. The whole Western world living on these four pillars. Just see our position. And the same conscious way, everyone is thinking, "If this movement goes on, then how all these nightclubs will go on? How all breweries will go on? How all slaughterhouse will go on, cigarette factories will go on?" This is all foolish. So you cannot expect that we will get more, many friends. That is not possible, because the world is full of Kamsas, demons.** So we have to struggle and... In the face of so many obstacles we have come to this standard that there is **one Hare Krishna movement; it is very dangerous to the modern way of life**. That much is great, advance. **They're feeling the pulse**. Now when they are meeting, state obstacles. Everywhere we are meeting obstacles. In Singapore

Pusta Krishna: We went to the airport.

Prabhupada: Yes.

Pusta Krishna: And practically they didn't even want to let us stay in the airport. We had to stay there only for four hours to catch the next flight. They are so much...
Prabhupada: This is our position. Gradually they will show Hare Krishna movement. In India also, although India's... **They will want to crush down this movement.** So this will be up to Him. Krishna or Krishna's movement, the same thing. And Krishna was attempted to be killed by Kamsa class of men and his company, the demons. **So it will be there; it is already there.** Don't be disappointed, because that is the meaning that it is successful.** Krishna's favor is there, because Krishna and Krishna's movement is not different, nondiff..., identical. So as Krishna was attempted to be killed, many, many years before He appeared... At eighth child, if the mother produces child yearly, still ten years, eight years before His birth, the mother was to be attempted to be killed. **So there may be attempt like that. And Lord Jesus Christ was killed. So they may kill me also.** *[Srila Prabhupada Room Conversation, May 3, 1976, Honolulu]*

Jesus was killed by the Jews. Prabhupada clearly knew this:

Prabhupada: **Yes, actually we can see that the Christians hate the Jews because the Jews crucified Christ.** They even utilize the symbol of the cross to remind people that the Jews crucified him. Even in the churches there are pictures of Lord Jesus, with thorns on his head, being forced to carry his cross. **In this way, the people are reminded of all the troubles that the Jews gave to Christ.** *[Dialectic Spiritualism Friedrich Wilhelm Nietzsche [1844-1900]*

So when Prabhupada said that "they may kill me also", this clearly indicates the same Jewish lineage that killed Christ.

Kamsa didn't wait for Krishna to appear to try to kill Him but he tried to kill His mother thinking he could check Krishna even appearing in this world. In the same way International Jewry knew that if Prabhupada's movement expanded, their plans for world domination would be finished. So they didn't wait to attempt to kill Prabhupada. We have to be assured on the strength of the above quote that like Kamsa the Jews wanted to cut Prabhupada down before he even got fully started. "Nip it in the bud".

Thus they would have planted some of their agents into ISKCON just before 1970 with the aim to first destroy the movement from within via divide and conquer.

The Protocols of The Learned Elders Of Zion

Goyim are mentally inferior to Jews and can't run their nations properly. For their sake and ours, we need to abolish their governments and replace them with a single government. This will take a long time and involve much bloodshed, but it's for a good cause. Here's what we'll need to do:

Place our agents and helpers everywhere

Take control of the media and use it in propaganda for our plans

Start fights between different races, classes and religions [Divide and Conquer] (Note: Tamal started fights between the different asramas or classes in ISKCON – see appendix 2)

We have agents placed everywhere, occupying many positions throughout society.

This way everyone will see how powerful we are; and they will be **in fear of our many international spies and agents who roam the earth without limitation.**

But how else were we to bring about that increase of trigger events **which lead to disorders within their administration?** ... Among those methods, one of the most important is **having agents for the restoration of order placed in such a way as to have the opportunity to cause problems. They will use their disintegrating activity to develop and display their evil inclinations** – obstinate self-conceit, irresponsible exercise of authority, and, first and foremost, an openness to bribery and corruption.

Being expert in this field, the Jews knew all too well that the best means to create divisions between Prabhupada and his young western disciples was to introduce the impersonal poison held by his deviant Godbrothers from the Gaudiya Math. Prabhupada clearly talks of this in the following quote:

GODBROTHERS THE POISON BUT NOT THE MANIPULATING SINISTER MOVEMENT

I am very pleased that you all GBC members are remaining vigilant so that the disturbance in our Society may not continue. In Isana and his wife's letters there is reference to Tirtha Maharaja's name, as if they were advised by Brahmananda Maharaja and company to come to India and join Tirtha Maharaja. It appears like that. I shall be glad if you kindly inquire on this point. **It is now clear that my Godbrothers take objection of my being called as Prabhupada and on this point they wanted to poison the whole Society--that is now clear. But how it was manipulated--that is a mystery.** *[Prabhupada Letter to: Rupanuga, Calcutta, 25 September, 1970]*

The poison is clearly the envy of Prabhupada's Godbrothers but the agents of the great sinister movement [Tamal and others] are the manipulators of that poison. That is indicated in the following letter:

I am very glad to know that the **GBC is actively working to rectify the subversive situation which has been weakening the very foundation of our Society.** All you members of the GBC please always remain very vigilant in this connection **so that our society's growth may go on unimpeded by such poisonous elements.** Your preaching in New Vrndavana as well as intensified study of our literatures with seriousness is very much encouraging. Please continue this program with vigor and reestablish the solidity of our movement.

From the very beginning I was strongly against the impersonalists and all my books are stressed on this point. So my oral instruction as well as my books are all at your service. Now you GBC consult them and get clear and strong idea, then there will be no disturbance. Disturbance is caused by ignorance; where there is no ignorance, there is no disturbance. **The four Sannyasis may bark, but still the caravan will pass. There is every evidence that they are influenced by some of my fourth-class Godbrothers.**

If there is opportunity, try to convince these rascal Sannyasis **who are misled by fourth-class men** that if they at all want to have a change of leadership why do they not select a better leader than at present moment. What is the use of finding out a fourth-class leader who has no asset as their background. I am simply sorry that such intelligent boys are misusing their brain-substance in this way. Try to rectify them as far as possible. **Isana Das has inquired from Tamala regarding Tirtha Maharaja. I do not know what is the sequence of this inquiry, but it is clear that there is a great clique and the so-called Sannyasis are the via media of spreading contamination in our Society. It is a very sorry plight.** [*Prabhupada Letter to: Hayagriva, Calcutta, 14 September, 1970*]

The poisonous contamination is impersonal philosophy which was spread into ISKCON via the four rascal Sannyasis, but it was done due to a great clique. [*Clique Meaning - A narrow circle of persons associated by common interests or for the accomplishment of a common purpose; -- generally used in a bad sense.*]

So the poison is the envious Godbrothers, the medium for getting that poison into ISKCON was the four bewildered Sannyasis [Brahmananda, Gargamuni, Visnujana and another maybe Subala] but the great clique [great sinister movement] which was organised by the Jewish agent Tamal, who is also mentioned in the above letter, was responsible for the manipulation of that poison into the society via subtle suggestions of association with the envious Godbrothers such as Tirtha Maharaja.

Tamal was a man so disturbing to Prabhupada's movement. He was always trying to create division in ISKCON, which is the goal of any agent planted by the Jews in an international movement that they wish to destroy from within. (Please See- APPENDIX 2 - Tamal's Divide & Conquer – on page 122) Tamal was so troublesome that His Divine Grace banished him to China [Tamal refused to go]. Later he was the chief culprit in a conspiracy to kill Prabhupada. Then after Prabhupada's departure he totally neglected Prabhupada's orders and hijacked the movement implementing unauthorized principles such as envious conditioned souls being worshiped as representatives of God. Are we really going to believe that Tamal's talks with Isana dasa and others in regards to Prabhupada's envious Godbrothers were to protect ISKCON? This reasoning is not very intelligent. Logic would strongly suggest Tamal's agenda was to manipulate poison into the society and thus cause division so he could conquer on behalf of the sinister movement.

Later in appendix 2 I will give interesting examples of Tamal's divisive behaviour. Now let us look in more detail in regards the impersonal contamination that poisoned these four sannyasis:

> Lately there has been some misunderstanding amongst our devotees about our Krishna Consciousness philosophy. Particularly there has been some confusion about the relationship between the Spiritual Master and Krishna. The Vedas say that there is a Master Krishna. This Servant Krishna is the Spiritual Master and this is the conclusion. **The Spiritual Master is the Mercy Representative of the Supreme Lord and as such He is given honor as good as Krishna, but He is never identical with Krishna.** Perhaps you know the picture of Madhvacarya, one of the great Acaryas in our line, who is holding two fingers up to indicate Krishna and jiva. The impersonalists hold up one finger because their idea is that everything is one. **So if we make the Spiritual Master identical with Krishna, then we will also become impersonalists. If we say that our Spiritual Master is Krishna, then the conclusion is that if we become Spiritual Master some day, then we will also become Krishna. Please try to understand how dangerous this kind of reasoning is.**
>
> In my books I have tried to explain clearly this simultaneously one and different philosophy acinta beda beda tattva propounded by Lord Caitanya Mahaprabhu. But sometimes it happens that this philosophy is given a self-interested interpretation. As soon as personal motivation comes in it is not possible for one to understand our Krishna Consciousness philosophy. [*Prabhupada Letter to: Isana, Vibhavati, Calcutta, 21 September, 1970*]

In regards to why you have been branded as Mayavadi sannyasi by society members, that is because you are identifying the Spiritual Master as God. We always represent ourselves as servant of God and you are preaching contrary. **The Spiritual Master should be given respect of God but that doesn't mean he is God. That is Mayavadi**. You should always remember that the Spiritual Master is the representative of God and should be given the respect of God **but that doesn't mean that he is God Himself!** You can speak of the Spiritual Master as "servant God" whereas Krishna is "master God". I think this is sufficient to clear the idea.

Regarding Swami Tirtha, this is just a rumor because in the past there where such symptoms. Now you should forget about the past, and go forward straight for preaching this Krishna Consciousness Movement. **Before preaching of your Spiritual Master as God, you never consulted me whether it was right. This means you were inspired by some external influence**. Subala said that it was a mystic influence. Why that was wasn't cleared up until now. That mystic influence was widely spread which I clearly saw in Honolulu, Tokyo or in other words, wherever Brahmananda went. Now we have to forget the past incidences and shall have to go forward with clear consciousness. *[Prabhupada Letter to: Gargamuni, Bombay, 27 October, 1970]*

Going back to the above discussion in which Prabhupada says the Jews may kill him:

So there may be attempt like that. And Lord Jesus Christ was killed. So they may kill me also. *[Srila Prabhupada Room Conversation, May 3, 1976, Honolulu]*

Even though International Jewry will have made several attempts to kill Prabhupada [via their Jewish agent Tamal], they were totally unsuccessful due to his being fully protected by Krishna [God]. Prabhupada only left this world under the direct guidance of the Lord when his work was done, not when the demons tried to kill him.

It cannot be checked. There may be so many hindrances. **But one who is pure devotee, his business cannot be stopped.** *[Srila Prabhupada from a Srimad Bhagavatam lecture 1.2.6. Calcutta. Feb 26th, 1974]*

Similarly, anyone who is ordered by the Lord to perform some action in this material world, especially preaching His glories, **cannot be counteracted by anyone**; the will of the Lord is executed under all circumstances. *[Srila Prabhupada from Srimad Bhagavatam 3.16.36]*

The Jews had no power to kill an exalted personality like Srila Prabhupada and they couldn't divide his movement during his physical presence. Thus they went from their failed internal divide and conquer to an external attack on the movement with deprogrammers.

PRABHUPADA PREDICTED THE ATTACK BY THE JEWS

Srila Prabhupada foresaw an attack on his movement coming from the Rabbis and the Christian priests. [Note: Christianity is now totally controlled by International Jewry].

But another thing, that **the priestly class of Christian and Jews churches, I think they are becoming envious of our movement.** Because they are afraid of their own system of religiosity, because they see so many young boys and girls are taking interest in this system of Krishna Consciousness. Naturally, they are not very satisfied. **So we may be facing some difficulty by them in future. So, we have to take some precaution.** Of course, this priestly class could not do anything very nice till now, but dogmatic way of thinking is going on. **So anyway, we shall have to depend on Krishna, and I think the new center in United Nations, if we make nice propaganda from there, then this tendency may be diminished.** In the United Nations center, I have already suggested Purusottama things to be done there, and if possible, we shall hold meeting and kirtana in the church center and distribute Prasadam, invite the prominent members of the United Nations, this is, I am thinking like that. I do not know what Krishna desires *[Prabhupada Letter to: Brahmananda 6 October, 1968]*

Prabhupada wanted to counteract this envious mentality by getting a preaching facility at the church center of the United Nations building in New York. This was checked by the demons.

In the next quote we see Prabhupada's prediction manifest with perfect accuracy. The internal divide and conquer had failed. The Hare Krishna movement was too strong during Prabhupada's physical presence. Now the Jews go full on with an external attack.

Just now there was a meeting of the five hundred leading rabbis of the Jewish faith in favor of deprogramming

Tamala Krishna: Just see. **They call a meeting of five hundred rabbis, all of the leading rabbis, and the Jewish leaders in the whole USA, just to deal with this question of "The cults taking our children."**

Prabhupada: (laughs) Us? Au…?

Tamala Krishna: Yes. We're the main cult.

Prabhupada: Then? This is a verse. They do not know what is the aim of life.

Hari-sauri: "Neither cleanliness nor proper behavior nor truth is found in them." All liars and cheats.

Prabhupada: **This is demon.**

Tamala Krishna: They're filthy. That's for sure. They are filthy. They have no idea of… In New York you can see that. They smell nasty. They keep on their shoes. You have to tell them to take… They never wash after eating. Even animals wash. At least they try to keep clean…..

Tamala Krishna: …kidnapped three of our devotees about a week before we… Just about a week…

Prabhupada: So we cannot take any position?

Tamala Krishna: Well, no, because the kidnapping is legal. They got…

Prabhupada: Then what can be done?

Tamala Krishna: They got permission from the court for conservatorship.

Adi-kesava: But two of the devotees have already escaped.

Prabhupada: If it is legal, what can I say?

Tamala Krishna: Yeah, that's… This is their new tactic now. This is their new tactic, that they're getting the court permission.

Prabhupada: **Then Americans' liberty is gone**.

Tamala Krishna: That's why the lawyers and others are very alarmed, the intellectuals, 'cause they're seeing it is becoming like Russia.

Adi-kesava: They're saying now that psychological freedom is more important in the law than religious freedom.

Prabhupada: Whatever it may be, if the law helps to kidnap, then what you can do?

Tamala Krishna: **He says that just now there was a meeting**

of the five hundred leading rabbis of the Jewish faith in favor of deprogramming, because they're very alarmed that the young men and women of the synagogues are joining our movement and other type of movements and leaving their so-called past religion. So the rabbis are going to take up... They like this deprogramming. They like this kidnapping. And he says also that just now in Newsweek magazine there's been a big article printed in favor of deprogramming, special article about this Tucson, Arizona, deprogramming center. **So he says that he expects more and more of this deprogramming.** He's a little bit alarmed because all of our leaders will be here in India now for the next few weeks.

Tamala Krishna: So he's a little alarmed that we'll all be coming to India, and these deprogrammers, they know this. So he's concerned.

Prabhupada: So do you think by going there they'll be saved?

Tamala Krishna: By staying in America, you mean?

Prabhupada: Hm.

Tamala Krishna: No.

Prabhupada: Then?

Adi-kesava: Most of the work that we can do doesn't have much to do with someone being taken, one person. It has to do with dealing with the whole issue. When we make...

Prabhupada: **No, how is this American law is allowed that anyone can be kidnapped?**

Tamala Krishna: Yes, that's the whole point...

Adi-kesava: We have gotten in some states injunctions from the court so that people cannot be taken. For instance in California they have an injunction. In Massachusetts...

Prabhupada: If this injunction is there, why don't you take steps and...?

Adi-kesava: They took them from other states. So we're trying to extend it now to the other states. But in some places there are new laws, so we have to find a new way to go against it. We have just defeated the law in the state of Vermont. They proposed one law...

Prabhupada: That law, but is what can I say?

Tamala Krishna: Yeah, no, I mean he wasn't asking for any statement. I was just giving it as information.

Prabhupada: That they have already taken. (converses with man in Bengali) (break) When there is fight, fight is fight. They'll take their tactics; we shall take our tactics.

Tamala Krishna: **You can see which groups are alarmed–the parents, the rabbis, and the priests.**

Prabhupada: **They should be alarmed. If Hare Krishna movement goes on, then their culture will be finished.**

[Room Conversation February 18, 1977, Mayapura]

DID PRABHUPADA CURSE INTERNATIONAL JEWRY FOR ATTACKING THE HARE KRISHNA MOVEMENT WITH DEPROGRAMMERS?

The attack by International Jewry on the Krishna consciousness movement was simultaneously an attack on Prabhupada and Lord Krishna Himself. So even though Prabhupada will be tolerant of any attack against himself, he will not tolerate Krishna being offended.

> Similarly, anger can be controlled. **We cannot stop anger altogether, but if we simply become angry with those who blaspheme the Lord or the devotees of the Lord, we control our anger in Krishna consciousness.** Lord Caitanya Mahaprabhu became angry with the miscreant brothers Jagai and Madhai, who blasphemed and struck Nityananda Prabhu. In His Siksastaka Lord Caitanya wrote, trnad api sunicena taror api sahisnuna: "One should be humbler than the grass and more tolerant than the tree." One may then ask why the Lord exhibited His anger. The point is that one should be ready to tolerate all insults to one's own self, but **when Krishna or His pure devotee is blasphemed, a genuine devotee becomes angry and acts like fire against the offenders**. *[Prabhupada from NOI Mantra 1]*

> This is our business. Because we are servants of God. **We cannot see anything blasphemy against God. That is not our business. We must chastise immediately.** *[Prabhupada Room Conversation July 7, 1976, Baltimore]*

At the same time Krishna will not tolerate any insult against His dear devotee Srila Prabhupada.

> **So this is the fact, that Krishna will never tolerate insult on a devotee. He will never tolerate.** The devotee may excuse, trnad api sunicena taror api sahisnuna. He may suffer. Just like Prahlada Maharaja, he was suffering. His father was torturing him. He was suffering, "All right." **But Krishna never tolerated. "Oh, you have done so much. Now it is the time to kill him." This is the process. Krishna will tolerate. Even**

you insult Krishna, He will tolerate. But if you insult His devotee, He will never tolerate. Then you are finished. Then you are finished. Just like a big man. If you insult him, he may think "All right, let him." But if you insult or do something harm to his child, he will never tolerate. He will never tolerate. **Similarly, a devotee who is dependent on Krishna in everything, and if somebody does harm to him, insults him, Krishna will never tolerate.** That is explained in the Caitanya-caritamrta, vaisnava-aparadha. Tara madhye vaisnava-aparadha hati matta. **So we should be very careful not to offend Vaisnava devotees. Not to offend. This is greatest offense.** Therefore it is said vipra-sapa-vimudhanam. Vimudhanam. **Those who are rascal, fools, they will want to try to insult real brahmana, Vaisnava. Then they are finished**. Of course, a Vaisnava never curses. Tolerates. Trnad api sunicena taror... Vaisnava tolerates, but Visnu never tolerates. *[Prabhupada Lecture Srimad-Bhagavatam 1.15.22-23, Los Angeles, December 2, 1973]*

PRABHUPADA'S CURSE

As stated in Bhagavad-gita (4.8), paritranaya sadhunam vinasaya ca duskrtam. The sadhus, the devotees of the Lord, are always eager to advance the cause of Krishna consciousness so that the conditioned souls may be released from the bondage of birth and death. But the asuras, the demons, impede the advancement of the Krishna consciousness movement, and therefore Krishna arranges occasional fights between different asuras who are very much interested in increasing their military power. The duty of the government or king is not to increase military power unnecessarily; the real duty of the government is to see that the people of the state advance in Krishna consciousness.... For flickering happiness, people waste their human energy, not understanding the importance of the Krishna consciousness movement **but instead accusing the simple devotees of brainwashing. Demons may falsely accuse the preachers of the Krishna consciousness movement, but Krishna will arrange a fight between the demons in which all their military power will be engaged and both parties of demons will be annihilated.** *[Prabhupada from Srimad Bhagavatam 9.24.59]*

Prabhupada: This is also arrangement by Krishna. Vinasaya ca duskrtam. "I will arrange soldiers. Russia will arrange for military power, America will arrange for military power, and they'll be engaged in fighting so that the overburdened earth will be released from these, all these demons. And it will pave the way for Krishna consciousness." And so long they're alive, they'll protest against Krishna consciousness: **"This is brainwash." So Krishna will arrange war between them. Then they'll be finished, and it will be easy for us to make progress.** So paritranaya sadhunam vinasaya ca duskrtam.

Satsvarupa: Why will that be favorable for us? You said that will be…

Prabhupada: Paritranaya sadhunam, that we are meeting so many obstacles for these rascal demons, and when they will be killed, then our path will be easier. And they will also understand that "This demonic way of life is not good. Let us take to Krishna." *[S.P. Morning Walk, January 28, 1977, Bhubaneshwar]*

International Jewry by their envious actions against Prabhupada and Krishna in the form of the Hare Krishna movement has a double curse on their heads.

THOSE WHO ARE ATTEMPTING
TO KILL, THEY WILL BE KILLED.

Therefore our movement is being checked in the Western countries that this is a brainwash movement. Brainwash movement, that we are injecting some ideas by psychology, mental control, and our people they are taking to it, and it is spreading like epidemic. How to check it? **Therefore they are now taking action how to stop this Hare Krishna movement in Europe and America.** They are trying. Of course, we are not afraid of this attempt. They will never be successful, rest assured, because we are pushing Krishna consciousness. Krishna was attempted to be killed from the very beginning of His life. That is the nature of this material world, "How to kill God," "God is dead." This is their attempt. So from the life of Krishna we can understand that so many attempts were made by the demons and the raksasas to kill Krishna, but actually Krishna killed them all. **So if you are sincere, if you follow the principles and push on this Krishna consciousness movement, nobody can kill you.** You'll go forward, rest assured. We are not going to be killed. That they are perceiving, that this movement is spreading like epidemic, and the young men of Europe and America, they're taking seriously. Professor

Stillson Judah already has given his conclusion that "This movement is not going to stop. It will go on." That's a fact. **Krishna cannot be killed, neither His movement cannot be killed. Rather, those who are attempting to kill, they will be killed**. But we must be very sincere, serious, follow the regulative principle and chant Hare Krishna mantra as you have been taught. Follow this principle boldly, and there is no fear. *[Prabhupada Lecture Srimad-Bhagavatam 5.5.32, Vrndavana, November 19, 1976]*

The following account is from the recently deceased devotee Pita das. It clearly confirms that the sinister movement now controlling ISKCON is international Jewry.

THE HARE KRISHNA MOVEMENT
NO LONGER A THREAT TO JUDAISM

"From 1983 to 1989 I was in Taipei Taiwan ROChina. First as an assistant to Sevananda Prabhu then as we were told we were not needed any longer and the GBC placed his students in the place of management. (to make a very long story short) I had to live outside teach ESL, English.

One day Srila Prabhupada from within my heart chaita guru sent a very young and attractive man and wife to me, at first they wanted to know where they could have lunch? They were not Chinese but European I recommended a pure veg place and we went to have lunch together.

They wanted to know everything about Krishna Consciousness. I had never met a more receptive couple in my life so much so that after lunch I invited them to my apartment on Yang Ming Mountain. After again speaking to them at least two more hours I finally asked them what did they think of Krishna Consciousness? They then said they were Jews born in a Jewish community in Cape Comeran in South India. Their parents had left Germany before the war. They then told me they taught English in Japan and were saving money because they wanted to live in Israel. They then explained that the Rabbis in Israel told them (and I quote them exactly):

THE HARE KRISHNA MOVEMENT WAS NO LONGER A THREAT TO JUDAISM because the Indian leader left his movement to his Jewish followers!

With my hands on Srila Prabhupada's lotus feet it happened just like that." Pita das

After hijacking ISKCON, the Jews may foolishly believe that the Hare Krishna Movement is no longer a threat to their plans for world domination. Unfortunately for them, true Krishna consciousness is not locked up in institutions controlled by demons. Rather it is found in the hearts of the pious. To protect those pious souls the Lord will establish the age of Satya (truth) for their spiritual enlightenment and annihilate the envious demons now ruling the world.

MORE CLEAR EVIDENCE

The following quote also confirms who are the most envious of Prabhupada's movement. In appendix 3 on page 137 you will find out very clearly who is behind communism. Also read again pages 70 to 80 to understand the non-human identity of the communist leaders who Prabhupada exposed as the GREAT SINISTER MOVEMENT in his ISKCON society.

Actually, everywhere envious people are against this movement, especially communists, because this movement is a threat to them

Our ultimate aim is to take part in politics, because Krishna took part in politics, we have to follow—but if people do not become Krishna conscious it won't be possible. Actually if we can take up the government, our movement will be very easily spread and beneficial to the people. We can make happy, peaceful men, God conscious—this is our aim. The main thing is to distribute books more and more. That remark by the man in Houston is to your credit, that this movement is becoming an epidemic. **Actually, everywhere envious people are against this movement, especially communists, because this movement is a threat to them**. The main thing is to distribute books—the communist idea is spread practically all over the world on account of distributing huge amounts of literature, but they have no substance.

[Srila Prabhupada Letter to: Balavanta, Vrindaban, 4 October, 1976]

Tamal's Divide & Conquer

In 1970 Srila Prabhupada claimed that the great sinister moment was now inside his ISKCON society. In appendix 1 called "THE GREAT SINISTER MOVEMENT CONTROLLING ISKCON" I presented evidence that this movement is international Jewry.

I also showed how societies like ISKCON are conquered from within by agents of the sinister movement via the method of divide and conquer. I also claimed that Tamal Krishna was clearly manifesting the traits of such an agent due to his divisive behaviour.

He totally cemented this position by trying to kill Srila Prabhupada. (Remember Prabhupada said "**Lord Jesus Christ was killed. So they may kill me also.**" The word **"they"** means international Jewry. Thus their agent for killing was clearly Tamal) After Prabhupada departed, Tamal hijacked ISKCON on behalf of international Jewry and introduced unauthorized principles designed to create disorder and division.

These are the main divisions that Tamal has fomented in the Vaishnava community:

1. ISKCON Diksa Gurus vs. The Ritviks
2. Prabhupada Book Changers vs. Advocates of Prabhupada's Original Unchanged Books.
3. The Flat Earthers vs. The Globe Earthers

You can approach any follower of Krishna consciousness and you will find that they have a view on all of the above topics. They will fall on one side or the other. Generally ISKCON devotees are fully on board with Tamal's deviations namely: ISKCON Diksa Gurus, changing Prabhupada's books and some form of flat earth or flat earth plane across the universe.

Thus we can see that without Tamal there would be no such division between devotees. Tamal has done his job as an agent of international Jewry and divided the movement via the introduction of apa-siddhantic conclusions. My business here is not to analyse these deviations that have caused such division, but to point out that Tamal was behind them. Thus Tamal, who was full on

Jew himself, named Thomas Herzig, fits perfectly the stereotypical inside agent for conquering over a movement that threatens international Jewry.

What I want to discuss now is the division that Tamal always tried to create between the different asramas in ISKCON, namely the grhasthas (householders) on one side and the brahmacaris (celibate students) and Sannyasis (renouned order) on the other.

This agenda first became clearly manifest in 1976, when Tamal was creating division between the grhasthas staying in the ISKCON temples of America and his Radha Damodar travelling sankirtana parties which mainly consisted of brahmacaris and Sannyasis.

Tamal was basically preaching that the real deal or best service for brahmacaris was to travel with his parties selling books. Staying in the temples and doing service with the grhasthas was maya or illusion. This was the not so subtle implication of Tamal's divisive preaching. Of course this agenda was implemented to take control of the movement by weakening the man-power in the temples thus making these temples harder to maintain. But it also created a division by making the householders like second class members of ISKCON. This was a classic divide and conquer tactic by Tamal.

This so much displeased Srila Prabhupada that he banished Tamal to China. It is described as follows in "Someone Has Poisoned Me" By: Nityananda Dasa and also by Gurukrpa dasa while speaking on ISKCON history:

"GO TO CHINA"

In TKG's (Tamal Krishna Gosvami) book, *A Hare Krishna at Southern Methodist University*, there is a chapter entitled *The Perils of Succession* wherein many of the controversial episodes of ISKCON history are clinically described, usually omitting the true details of Tamal's own role in or orchestration of such controversies. One such event was the Radha Damodar travelling parties which Tamal controlled in 1976. Srila Prabhupada became so upset with Tamal's conduct of creating great disturbance in the USA ISKCON centers that His Divine Grace relieved Tamal of all services and responsibilities, ordering him to go to China. Tamal resisted and Srila Prabhupada became angry with him, and held fast to Tamal's "banishment" behind the Yellow Curtain. It was clear that by this event, Tamal was disgraced, humiliated, and severely chastised before the entire assemblage of devotees at the annual Mayapur festival, 1976. Adi Keshava agrees that the affair made Tamal very resentful towards Srila Prabhupada.

After the 1976 Mayapur festival, Tamal and Dristadyumna studied about China and prepared a report for Srila Prabhupada. In a meeting with Srila Prabhupada in Hawaii on May 4, 1976, Tamal submitted the bleak report and described how the only method of distributing books in China would be to throw sealed, floating bags of books into the ocean, hoping they would wash ashore and be found by coastal residents. Dristadyumna and Tamal attended a book publisher's convention undercover on mainland China for a few days. Tamal reported to Srila Prabhupada that there was absolutely no way to preach in China, *"maybe in fifty years (from now)."* Srila Prabhupada excused Tamal of the order to go to China, and returned Tamal to his former position as head of the Radha Damodar bus program. Tamal soon afterwards assumed the GBC position for New York zone as well. Adi Keshava described Tamal's return to New York as pompous and *triumphant*.

While in New York, Tamal wrote and supervised the production of a play done by Sudama Swami and the devotee actors. It was an obvious indulgence in TKG's personal and emotional history of banishment and chastisement by Srila Prabhupada. The play was entitled *"The Emperor and His Chief Counselor."* The counselor created havoc in the emperor's kingdom, is chastised, and realizing his mistake, repented and became re-situated properly in the service of the emperor once again. Adi Keshava, however, thought the play was frightening and bizarre, being all about court intrigue, pride, power, and how Tamal had been wrongly chastised because although he had overstepped his bounds with abuse of the counselor's position, he had done so with only good intentions.

["Someone Has Poisoned Me" By: Nityananda Dasa]

Question: How did Tamal Krsna Swami become so influential at this time?

Gurukrpa: Tamal's original service was as GBC in India. He left that service without permission and arrived in America. **Within one year the temple presidents made a huge complaint to Prabhupada that he was disrupting the**

temples by taking important men. I was in the room when Prabhupada told Tamal to go to China. Hari Sauri's memory of this incident is not accurate. Either way that is another story.

Tamal went to New York to prepare to go to China. And in May 1976, he showed up in a suit in Honolulu, a broken man. He could not get a visa to China, he had no service to do in India, and he could not go back to America, so he was quite depressed. Approximately a day or two later, Prabhupada called for Tamal and me at about 12:30 AM. He said, "My feet are swelling, my teeth are getting loose, I am passing urine too frequently. These are the first signs that death is coming." Then he sent us back to bed. The next day Tamal volunteered to be Prabhupada's secretary, as the service was vacant at that time. **From this position he could control and manipulate the environment around Srila Prabhupada. I can write many more stories that will shock people about Tamal's ambitious nature and his desire to take Prabhupada's seat.**

[Gurukrpa das speaks on ISKCON History]

MADHUDVISA EXPOSES TAMAL

Now I wish to look in detail at a conversation in which Tamal is exposed for again creating division between the grhastha's and brahmacari's/Sannyasis. It appears that Madhudvisa prabhu had reported Tamal to Prabhupada for his envious and divisive activities.

Prabhupada: ...telling that too much stricture on the grhasthas may cause some disturbance. Eh?

Madhudvisa: Yes.

Note: Later in this conversation Prabhupada describes this disturbance as a faction causing division between everyone. Prabhupada requests that this attitude should not be brought into ISKCON. We will now clearly see who was behind such opposition to Prabhupada's authority.

Prabhupada: So I think the grhastha themselves should form a small committee and define what they will do, instead of forcing something, because in this age, nobody can follow strictly all the stricture in the sastras.

Tamala Krsna: I don't think that we formulated anything for them to do.

Note: Prabhupada rebukes the so called high and mighty "sannyasis & brahmacaris" by saying nobody can strictly follow all the stricture in the sastra. Thus we can understand from Prabhupada's statement that Tamal is being fanatical by trying to force things onto the grhasthas. He was trying to stigmatize them from his imagined position of superiority and thus create division in ISKCON.

Just look at the impudence of Tamal! Here he directly challenges Prabhupada. This is not the attitude of a humble servant of the spiritual master but the attitude of an arrogant demon.

Prabhupada: Hm?

Tamala Krsna: Any of our resolutions, it doesn't say anything about what they should do. It simply says what should, how our society should be run, our temples. It doesn't state anything about how the grhasthas should live.

Note: Again Tamal defies Prabhupada and tries to deny he is a fanatic causing division between devotees. Prabhupada now asks Madhudvisa prabhu to reaffirm his complaint against Tamal.

Prabhupada: No... What? What, was your pro...?

Madhudvisa: Well, last evening we were saying that sex life according to the regulative principles means sex life only when the guru tells the grhastha to have sex life. And what I said last night is that if that is the case, then there would be no more grhasthas in the society. They will not... They will not become grhasthas.

Prabhupada: Be practical.

Devotees: Laughter

Note: Here Prabhupada clearly exposes Tamal as a fanatic who is causing disunity by trying to impose impractical rules on the grhasthas.

Tamala Krsna: So that point they can discuss amongst themselves, but that doesn't have anything to do with our resolutions. Right?

Devotee: Yeah. This is the idea.

Prabhupada: Hm?

Tamala Krsna: In other words, our resolutions are on another point, that as far as when they, when they have sex life and when they don't, they should have a committee and they can decide that. But... Resolutions we passed have nothing to do with that. Our resolutions had to do with if someone is not to be supported by the movement, things like this. Those things are a different matter. The actual way the grhasthas should live, that is their... They should decide that by committe.

Note: Again Tamal tries to deny the accusations that are made against him by Madhudvisa. If the claims of Madhudvisa were wrong, Prabhupada would not waste his time addressing them. The claims against Tamal were factual and disturbing to the society.

Yasodanandana: There now should be a proposition that before they enter the grhastha asrama, they should have a means of supporting themselves besides the living off the society.

Tamala Krsna: That was said...

Yasodanandana: They would...

Tamala Krsna: Those things, the GBC made a resolution...

Madhudvisa: The resolutions that we made were wrong in that regard.

Tamala Krsna: Ah?

Madhudvisa: The resolutions that we made were wrong. Prabhupada rectified us.

Tamala Krsna: In what regard?

Note: Tamal is again in denial mode. He is saying the GBC resolutions that he was behind, were not imposing any rules on the way grhasthas should live. Madhudvisa exposes his argument by stating that Prabhupada had to rectify those wrong resolutions.

Madhudvisa: We made a resolution that if a householder gets married, then he has to take care of his wife for the rest of his life till he takes sannyasa.

Tamala Krsna: Yeah, Prabhupada corrected that.

Madhudvisa: Yeah. So that resolution was wrong.

Tamala Krsna: So?

Madhudvisa: And also the resolution about the women and the children coming to the temple, not accepting them, that was also wrong.

Tamala Krsna: So now what's the point?

Madhudvisa: So now they're rectified.

Tamala Krsna: So now what is the point?

Madhudvisa: I'm just saying that we should have a more practical understanding of this, of our attitude towards the whole situation.

Tamala Krsna: That's why Prabhupada corrected us.

Note: Prabhupada corrected you so your resolutions were wrong! THIS IS THE CLEAR POINT. Just look at this arrogant rascal. Even after Madhudvisa exposes him he tries to wash it off as nothing. Tamal is clearly creating division in the society by his fanatical behaviour and he tries to bluff his way out of the situation by giving up all accountability. It's like he's saying: "So what if I did that. Prabhupada corrected me, so it's alright. I can do whatever nonsense I like. I am above the law."

Prabhupada: So I think it may be further decided. Make a small committee of three or four grhasthas, and you define how you live.

Note: Here Prabhupada takes away all Tamal's power to mess around with the way grhasthas should live. The grhasthas will decide things for themselves not Tamal and the GBC.

Tamala Krsna: Well, what about their relationship with the society? This point was to... I don't understand why that is being avoided. In other words, how they should live, that they should have a committee for, but the fact that the society cannot support them, that is not for them to decide. That is for the GBC to decide. That is my point.

Yasodanandana: I think that point, that's clear.

Prabhupada: Hm?

Tamala Krsna: As far as their living conditions, so let them have a committee.

Madhudvisa: Yeah. I agree with that.

Tamala Krsna: All right. Then there's no disagreement. As long as you say we should not disclaim all of our resolutions.

Madhudvisa: No, no, no, no.

Tamala Krsna: Oh, then it's all right.

Jayapataka: Srila Prabhupada is so merciful that if it comes to a point where it means that a person is not in Krsna consciousness or in Krsna consciousness, I think Prabhupada'd rather support them and let them be Krsna conscious. That's why you have to see whether they stay in the society.

Note: Good lip service Jayapataka. Yes Prabhupada wants to support the grhasthas while Tamal and company wants to castigate and banish them to an inferior position in ISKCON.

Pusta Krsna: Dragging us back to Godhead.

Prabhupada: When this pandal is going to be filled up?

Bhavananda: The exhibits should be arriving today with the devotees, Prabhupada.

Prabhupada: Who are these men?

Bhavananda: They are the pandal workers.

Prabhupada: Pandal work... (break) Always, what is called...? Communism. They say, whole world, "We are Communists," "We are capitalists," "We are socialists," and "We are nonviolent," "We are violent."

Madhudvisa: Dualism.

Prabhupada: Eh?

Madhudvisa: Dualism?

Prabhupada: Yes. Not dualism. How many isms, nobody knows. But... What is called? Faction. Faction. Everyone is divided from the other.

Madhudvisa: Yeah.

Prabhupada: So we should not bring that attitude in our society. That is my request.

Note: This is the point I mentioned above. Tamal is clearly the person responsible for the faction making everyone divided. He is the one bringing this attitude in Prabhupada's society because he is the agent of the great sinister movement.

Guru-krpa: Envious. They're all envious.

Note: Guru-krpa nails it! They're the envious dressed as devotees in the Krishna consciousness movement that Prabhupada mentioned we should completely neglect. (See Caitanya Caritamrta Madhya Lila 1.218)

Prabhupada: That you should not do. And that unity is possible with, only when harer nama is there constantly. Otherwise, it will be factional. What do you call? Factional is the right word?

Hamsaduta: Yes, yes. Factional.

Pusta Krsna: What about the distinction between the enjoying spirit and the renouncing spirit?

Prabhupada: Hm?

Pusta Krsna: For example, there is, as we have been discussing, there is between the brahmacaris and the grhasthas... The brahmacaris have this tendency--at least, this is the attitude-- towards renunciation. And so far we can see, a brahmacari who gives up his brahmacari life means he's more inclined towards the enjoying spirit, at least to some extent. So how do we deal with this situation?

Prabhupada: You can... If you want to enjoy, who can stop you?

Tamala Krsna: But we cannot..., we cannot support it. We cannot support his enjoyment. That he should take on his own self to do.

Prabhupada: They... According to different position and attitude, the four asramas are there: brahmacari, grhastha, vanaprastha, sannyasa. This means that everyone is not on the equal platform. Different platform. But the whole idea is how to give up the propensity of enjoyment. That is wanted.

Note: Not everyone is on the same platform but all the different asramas work to give up the propensity for material enjoyment. But irresponsible men who cannot be honest and become grhasthas but instead take the position of sexyasis* are actually in the lowest platform far below the honest grhasthas who they harass out of their envy.

Pusta Krsna: We find in the Srimad Bhagavatam that Sukadeva Gosvami would approach the householders in the morning just so long as to give them a little bit of spiritual knowledge, and he would accept the offering of some milk. So the sannyasis and renunciates, generally, they wouldn't very much relish the association of householders because of this enjoying spirit and the association that it entails. So we're finding also within our society that those who are inclined towards remaining celibate, they're finding the association of persons even within our movement who have this enjoying spirit to be somewhat detrimental to their own spiritual life.

Guru-krpa: Grhe thako vanete thako...

Note: Again Guru-krpa nails it. Whatever position one holds, one should always remember Krishna. Grhastha is no impediment. Prabhupada says "So Bhaktivinode Thakura advises, grhe thako, vane thako, sada 'hari' bole' dako. Grhe thako means either you stay at your home as a householder, or you stay in the forest as the renounced order of life, it does not make difference, but you have to chant the maha-mantra, Hare Krsna." Purport to Gay Gaura Madhur Sware.

*Footnote - Men with sex desire are not "sannyasis" and wives not devoted to their husbands, are not wives. They both have only half a body. New names have to be invented for these two groups of Kali-yuga disciples. These are our suggestions. Men who are too immature to get married, but are still full of sex desire and so need a stick to carry around with them so they can be respected, should be called "sexyasis." Women who hate men, and would rather live on welfare, or would rather devote themselves to a sexyasi than their husbands, may be called "sexyasinis." Sulocana Prabhu from the GURU BUSINESS

Prabhupada: Then. What is your proposal? They should go away?

Note: Here Prabhupada reveals the actual objectives of these sexyasis like Tamal. They want to drive away all the sincere honest devotees of the Lord and build a fake society based on name, fame and adoration (subtle sex). This they have now done. The whole of ISKCON now has its foundations in unalloyed illicit sex. This is described by Sulocana Prabhu in his Guru Business: "Woman claiming to have a relationship with one of these "ISKCON" sexyasis should know, without a doubt, that such a relationship is nothing but unalloyed illicit sex, which will destroy any possibility of a successful marriage."

Madhudvisa: Unless there is association, then they will never become purified.

Tamala Krsna: Who says they won't asso...? What is this discussion? This is not...

Madhudvisa: It's not a resolution.

Tamala Krsna: This is not a good discussion either.

Pusta Krsna: No, but this is basically the problem.

Tamala Krsna: No, it's not the problem, because everyone comes together in a temple for kirtana, for lectures, for prasadam. These things are common activities. There's no question that we should not have common activities between all the asramas. These are the common ac... But for living, there must be separate arrangement.

Prabhupada: Now, even in the temple, you were complaining, the husband and wife were talking.

Note: Here Prabhupada exposes the envy of Tamal. He cannot even tolerate the grhasthas talking with each other in the temples.

Tamala Krsna: Yes. That's living. That means living. That is not... They're not talking Srimad Bhagavatam.

Prabhupada: That... (break)......

Bhagavata: About attraction and aversion... There's...

Prabhupada: Hm? Attraction?

Bhagavata: ...a point about attraction and aversion, that there's a complaint that sometimes there's too much aversion on the part of the brahmacaris. But isn't that not a quality, to a point a brahmacari should have a healthy contempt for sense gratification?

Prabhupada: I do not follow.

Pusta Krsna: He's saying that sometimes the brahmacaris, even the sannyasis, they may have a very strong aversion towards association with women and.or householder life, things of this nature. And sometimes the grhasthas will criticize the sannyasis and brahmacaris that "This is fanaticism," or it's, to the other end, "It's just as bad as the enjoying spirit, because you're meditating on the same thing, but only you're averse to it." So what is the...? Bhagavata dasa's question is "What is the condition?" Is it better to be neutral or to be averse?

Tamala Krsna: Neutral.

Note: Good lip service from Tamal but his actions show that he is far from neutral. Tamal displays strong aversion to the grhasthas who he envies and wishes to isolate. This is how he divides so he can conquer for his masters in the sinister movement.

Prabhupada: These are all fanaticism. Real unity is in advancing Krsna consciousness. Kalau nasty eva nasty eva... In Kali-yuga, you cannot strictly follow, neither I can strictly follow. If I criticize you, if you criticize me, then we go far away from our real life of Krsna consciousness.

Note: Those who have followed Tamal and not Prabhupada are fanatics who have gone far away from real Krishna consciousness.

Pusta Krsna: So is it correct to say that if we're not Krsna conscious, then if it's not the grhastha problem, it would be some other problem?

Prabhupada: Yes.

Pusta Krsna: We'll find something or another to absorb our time with besides Krsna.

Prabhupada: No, you should always remember that either grhastha or brahmacari or sannyasi, nobody can strictly follow all the rules and regulations of them. In the Kali-yuga it is not possible. So if I find simply fault with you, and if you find fault with me, then it will be factional, and our real business will be hampered. Therefore Caitanya Mahaprabhu has recommended that hari-nama, chanting Hare Krsna mantra, should be very rigidly performed, which is common for everyone: grhastha, vanaprastha or sannyasi. They should always chant Hare Krsna mantra. Then everything will be adjusted. Otherwise it is impossible to advance. We shall be complicated with the details only. This is called niyamagrahah. I think I have explained.

Note: So Tamal's business of finding fault with the grhasthas was simply creating factions and hampering the real business of Krishna consciousness. But ultimately that was his job as the agent of international Jewry.

Madhudvisa: In the Nectar of Instruction.

Prabhupada: Niyamagrahah is not good. Niyama means regulative principles. And niyama-agrahah is niyamagrahah. Agrahah means not to accept. And niyama-agraha. Agraha means only eager to follow the regulative principles, but no advancement spiritually. Both of them are called niyamagrahah. So the basic principle is that niyamagrahah is not recommended. The real business is that.... And if we advance in Krsna consciousness, simple method, chanting twenty-four hours, kirtaniyah sada harih, then things will be automatically adjusted. You cannot find in Kali-yuga everything is being done very correctly, to the point. That is very difficult. Just like our poet, Allens Ginberg. He was always accusing me, "Swamiji, you are very conservative and strict." Actually, I told him that "I am never strict, neither I am conservative. If I become conservative, then I cannot live here for a moment. So I'm not at all conservative." (laughter) I was cooking, and I saw in the, what is called, refrigerator of Yeargen, Yeargon? What is his...?

Tamala Krsna: Yeah. Jergen. That boy you were staying with.

Prabhupada: Ah, ah! I saw he kept some pieces of meat for his cat. So still, I kept my things in that refrigerator. What can be done? I had no place at that time. Jaya. (break)

[Morning Walk, March 10, 1976, Mayapur]

TKG - TAMAL KRISHNA GOSWAMI'S HISTORY TIMELINE

* 1968 TKG said that "arsenic is a poison" (that cannot be detected) to Srila Prabhupada.

* 1971 TKG insisted on taking sannyasa and pestered Srila Prabhupada on this point (sannyasis are given high resepct).

* 1971 Nara Narayana Visvakarma das hears Tamal say that Srila Prabhupada is "a senile old man."

* TKG was the last person seen talking to Vishnujana and Gopijanaballabha, both of whom are reported to have commited suicide. Braja also tried to kill himself by beating himself on the head with a hammer -- after talking to Tamal. There are allegations that others tried to commit suicide due to the influence of Tamal.

* 1976 TKG started a war against the householders (varnasrama). TKG tried to move them out of the temples and to Australia. Srila Prabhupada had to stop this and he was very upset with Tamal.

* 1976 TKG tried to takeover ISKCON by draining manpower from the temples. Srila Prabhupada responded by saying TKG should be sent to China. TKG refused to go. Srila Prabhupada had to stop this and he was very upset with Tamal. Was TKG developing a grudge against Srila Prabhupada for blocking his takeover attempts?

* May 27, 1977 TKG and Bhavananda inform Srila Prabhupada that many (GBC) men will try to pose as guru after he departs. Srila Prabhupada warns them to "vigilantly manage" that this will not occur.

* May 28, 1977 Srila Prabhupada confirms that he is not going to appoint any guru successors. However, just after he departed, TKG said that Srila Prabhupada had appointed eleven gurus -- on May 28th 1977?

* May 30, 1977 Sudama said that Tamal and Bhavananda offered him "a piece of the pie." "Tommorow we are going to divide up the world."

* June 1977 TKG refused to allow all the devotees to come to India (afraid they might ask questions about guru succession)?

* November 1977 TKG refused to allow Srila Prabhupada on parikrama, despite that Srila Prabhupada said this would cure his illness.

* November 1977 TKG told Satsvarupa that Srila Prabhupada had wanted us to give him something to make him die. (Isa dasa has the audio of this on his website). Tamal: "A number of times he (Srila Prabhupada) would say: "Can you give me a medicine, please give me medicine, that will allow me to disappear now." At other times ..."I want most to disappear ...I want to die."* November 1977, declares that he is Srila Prabhupada's guru successor.

* November 1978, TKG begins to say that he is the exclusive "guru shakti" of Srila Prabhupada and he is better than all of the rest of the GBC combined.

* 1980 TKG admits that the GBC's "guru appointment" is a hoax.

* 1980 TKG admits that he was accused of killing Srila Prabhupada. (SHPM p.390)

* 1981 TKG tells his followers that Bhavananda (a homosexual) is his favorite of all of the GBC's "gurus."

*1985 TKG "kicks out" of Dallas a woman who was complaining that her children were being molested (Guruvastakam: Diane Stercowitz).

* 1986 TKG helps reinstate a known homosexual pedophile as a guru.

Who Is Behind Communism?

Srila Prabhupada is very clear in regards to who the demoniac people behind communism are.

> Ramesvara: These banks in the West, they supported Lenin. They made it possible to finance his revolution.
>
> Prabhupada: **Yes. They have got money. The Jews have got money. They want to invest and get some profit. Their only interest is how to get money, no nationalism, no religion, nothing of the sort. Therefore it is not now; long, long ago... Therefore Shakespeare wrote "Shylock, the Jew."**
>
> Hari-sauri: Yes. "Shylock."
>
> Prabhupada: "One pound of flesh." **The Jews were criticized long, long ago**.
>
> Hari-sauri: They were hated in the Middle Ages.
>
> *(Conversation, January 23, 1977, Bhubaneswar)*

No nationalism, no religion, nothing of the sort. The Jews only interest is in money with which to gain power and control of the earth. This is the nature of the demon described by the Lord in the Bhagavad-gita.

> The demoniac person thinks: "So much wealth do I have today, and I will gain more according to my schemes. So much is mine now, and it will increase in the future, more and more. He is my enemy, and I have killed him; and my other enemy will also be killed. I am the lord of everything. I am the enjoyer. I am perfect, powerful and happy. I am the richest man, surrounded by aristocratic relatives. There is none so powerful and happy as I am. I shall perform sacrifices, I shall give some charity, and thus I shall rejoice." In this way, such persons are deluded by ignorance. *(Bhagavad-gita 16.13-15)*

In the book The Myth of German Villainy by Benton L. Bradberry, there is the following section that shows very clearly who is behind the communist revolution to convert the world to Godlessness.

"Anthony C. Sutton wrote in his book, "Wall Street and the Bolshevik Revolution," New Rochelle, 1974: *"A number of very wealthy Jews in Wall Street firms contributed to the Communist regime during its early years when it was already soaked with the blood of innocent people who were being killed, exiled and expropriated simply because of their former class status. The largely Jewish government was taking a terrible vengeance against those who had prospered in the days of the Czars. The Wall Street capitalists were aiding the mostly Jewish rulers of Russia in a government dedicated to the overthrow of capitalism is vivid proof of the solidarity of a race with a long record of being perpetual aliens, no matter in what land they happened to be residing. Blood is thicker than water."* Jews comprised less than 2 percent of the Russian population, yet they now had total control of every branch of the government as well as the armed forces.

Jews in the Government of Bolshevik Russia

According to British newspaperman Robert Wilton, in his book, "The Last Days of the Romanovs," 1920, the Bolshevik government in Russia was totally dominated by Jews. Wilton had been The Times of London's man-in-Moscow from 1902 through 1919 and was in position to witness everything that happened in the revolution and who was behind it, and he regularly reported back on it. Wilton was in Russia during her shocking defeat in the Russo-Japanese War of 1904-05, through all the stresses and strains of internal Russian politics, the violent Potemkin and Bloody Sunday events of 1905, and the ominous revolutionary activities, from exile, of Lenin and Trotsky. He was there through the Great War of 1914-1918 (WWI) and witnessed the chaotic conditions that followed. He witnessed and reported on the Russian Revolution. He knew the facts as few others did. He knew and reported the fact that it was the Jews who were behind the revolution and the Jews who had taken over the Russian state.

In 1919, the Soviet Press provided a list of 556 important figures of the Soviet Government identifying their ethnicity. Wilton obtained this list and reported it back to London. He also included it as an "appendix' in his book, "The Last Days of the Romanovs," 1920, of which this author has a copy. The list included 17 Russians, 2 Ukrainians, 11 Armenians, 35 Letts, 15 Germans, 1 Hungarian 10 Georgians, 3 Poles, 3 Finns, 1 Czech, 1 Karaim (Jewish sect) and **457 Jews**. (The full list is provided starting on page 79 of Benton Bradberry's book), so there can be no refuting the fact that Jews dominated the Communist government of the Soviet Union.

It has often been noted that Jews are the only ethnic group who routinely change their names. One of their methods of gaining power and control is to insinuate themselves into high office "insidiously," while concealing the fact that they are Jewish. Adopting a Russian name in Russia or an English name in America is done for that purpose. That accounts for the adoption of different names by so many of the Jewish Bolsheviks involved in the Russian revolution.

According to Albert Lindemann, in his book "Esau's Tears, Modern Anti-Semitism and the Rise of the Jews," 1997, several of the leading non-Jews in the Bolshevik movement, including Lenin might be termed *"Jewified non-Jews."* For example, he writes, *"Lenin openly and repeatedly praised the role of Jews in the revolutionary movement."* He was married to a Jew, spoke Yiddish and his children spoke Yiddish. Lenin once said, *"An intelligent Russian is almost always a Jew or someone with Jewish blood in their veins."* Even if he was only one fourth Jew, Lenin lived as a Jew and surrounded himself with Jews.

A British Government White Paper, of April, 1919 stated: *"It was an open secret that the overthrow of the Russian Government and the seizure of power with incalculable consequences for the rest of the world was largely organized by international Jewish revolutionaries. The world's greatest land mass was being hi-jacked."*

Mr. M. Oudendyke, the Representative of the Netherlands Government in St. Petersburg, who was in charge of British interests after the liquidation of the British Embassy by the Bolsheviks, sent in a report to Foreign Secretary Sir Arthur Balfour.

"I consider that the immediate suppression of Bolshevism is the greatest issue now before the world, not even excluding the war which is still raging, and unless Bolshevism is nipped in the bud immediately it is bound to spread in one form or another over Europe, and the whole world, as it is organized and worked by Jews, who have no nationality, and whose one object is to destroy for their own ends the existing order of things."

Winston Churchill agreed with this view, in an article he wrote for the "Illustrated Sunday Herald," Feb. 8, 1920: *"It may well be that this same astounding race (Jews) may at the present time be in the actual process of providing another system of morals and philosophy, as malevolent as Christianity was benevolent, which if not arrested, would shatter irretrievably all that Christianity has rendered possible. This movement among the Jews is not new. It has been the mainspring of every subversive movement during the nineteenth century; and now at last this band of extraordinary personalities from the underworld of the great cities of Europe and America have gripped the Russian people by the hair of their heads and have become practically the undisputed masters of that enormous empire."*

Hilaire Belloc wrote in the "British G.K. Weekly," on February 4, 1937: *"As for anyone who does not know that the present revolutionary movement is Jewish in Russia, I can only say that he must be a man who is taken in by the suppression of our despicable Press."*

Even the Jews did not deny it. An article in the "Jewish Chronicle" on April 4, 1919 stated: *"The conceptions of Bolshevism are in harmony in most points with the ideas of Judaism.''*

In his book, "The Jewish Century," Yuri Sliezkine describes the astonishing rise of Jews to elite status in all areas of Soviet society after the revolution -- in culture, the universities, professional occupations, the media, and government. Sliezkine, a Russian Jew himself, immigrated to America in 1983 and became a professor at U.C. Berkeley "After the revolution," he wrote, *"millions of Jews left the shtetl towns of Russia to move to Moscow and other Russian cities, to take up elite positions in the new Soviet state"*

Claire Sheridan, the notorious cousin of Winston Churchill, and a well known sculptress, and friend of Leon Trotsky, travelled to Russia in the autumn of 1920 to create sculptures of prominent Bolsheviks, including Lenin, Trotsky, Dzerzhinsky and Kamenev. She said, *"The Communists are Jews, and Russia is being entirely administered by them. They are in every government office. They are driving out the Russians. "*

The Jewish Chronicle of January 6, 1933 stated: *"Over one-third of Jews in Russia have become officials."*

M. Cohen wrote, in "The Communist," April 12, 1919: *"The great Russian revolution was indeed accomplished by the hands of the Jews. There are no Jews in the ranks of the Red Army as far as privates are concerned, but in the Committees, and in the Soviet organizations ' Commissars, the Jews are gallantly leading the masses. The symbol of Jewry has become the symbol of the Russian proletariat, which can be seen in the fact of the adoption of the five-pointed star, which in former times was the symbol of Zionism and Jewry. "*

Adriana Tyrkova-Williams, in her book, "From Liberty to Brest-Litovsk," McMillan, 1919 wrote: *"There are few Russians among the Bolshevist wire-pullers, i.e. few men imbued with the all-Russian culture and interests of the Russian people. None of them have been in any way prominent in any stage of former Russian life...Besides obvious foreigners, Bolshevism recruited many adherents from among emigres who had spent many years abroad. Some of them had never been to Russia before. They especially numbered a great many Jews. They spoke Russian badly. The nation over which they had seized power was a stranger to them, and besides, they behaved as invaders in a conquered country. Throughout the revolution generally and Bolshevism in particular, the Jews occupied a very influential position. This phenomenon is both curious and complex.*   *"*

An article in a widely known French journal, "L'Illustration," of September 14, 1918, carried this comment: *"When one lives in constant contact with the functionaries who are serving the Bolshevik Government, one feature strikes the attention, which is that almost all of them are Jews. I am not at all anti-Semitic; but I must state what strikes the eye: everywhere in Petrograd, in Moscow, in provincial districts, in commissariats, in district offices, in Smolny, in the Soviets, 1 have met nothing but Jews and again Jews."*

And this, in a speech by Adolf Hitler, September, 1937: *"In 1936 we proved by means of a whole series of astounding statistics that in Russia today more than 98% of the leading positions are occupied by Jews... Who were the leaders in our Bavarian Workers Republic? Who were the leaders of the Spartacist Movement? Who were the real leaders and financiers of the Communist Party? Jews, every one of them. The position was the same in Hungary and in the Red parts of Spain."*

And Churchill, again, in an article he wrote for the "Illustrated Sunday Herald," in London, on February 8, 1920: *"There is no need to exaggerate the part played in the creation of Bolshevism and in the actual bringing about of the Russian Revolution by these international, and for the most part, atheistical, Jews. It is certainly a very great one, it probably outweighs all others. With the notable exception of Lenin [Lenin was 1/4 Jew, spoke Yiddish and had a Jewish wife], the majority of the leading figures are Jews. Moreover, the principal inspiration and driving power comes from the Jewish leaders... In the Soviet institutions the predominance of Jews is even more astounding. And the principal part in the system of terrorism applied by the extraordinary Commissions for combating Counter-Revolution (Cheka) has been taken by Jews..."*

Proof of the Jewish nature of the Russian Revolution and of the preponderance of Jews in the Bolshevik government, as well as their role in the Communist revolutions which swept Europe afterwards, is irrefutable. Nevertheless, one will not find this information in modern text books in either American or European universities. No scholar may state these facts or write them in a book ii he hopes to have his book published and promoted in the mainstream publishing industry, or if he hopes to have a career as a scholar. No politician dares utter these facts if he hopes to remain a politician. The only permissible story is that the Jews are now and always have been Western Christian Civilization's blameless victims. To say otherwise makes one an anti-Semite, worthy only to be cast out of civilized society. This is the nature of Jewish power." (The Myth of German Villainy by Benton L. Bradberry - Chapter Four)

THE JEWISH RED TERROR

After taking full control of Russia, these demons started to rain down the most horrific terror on the population, especially the Christian people. (Note: Please read chapter five called Red Terror in The Myth of German Villainy by Benton L. Bradberry)

Prabhupada said that the Jewish Bolsheviks (especially led by Stalin) were the greatest criminals in the history of the world.

Just like in the Communist country the Stalin was their dictator. And in the historical record it is said that he is the greatest criminal in the history of the world. Greatest criminal. *[Prabhupada Lecture, Bhagavad-gita 1.4, London, July 10, 1973]*

This is confirmed by Aleksandr Solzhenitsyn the Russian novelist, philosopher, historian, and political prisoner as follows.

You must understand, the leading Bolsheviks who took over Russia were not Russians. They hated Russians. They hated Christians. Driven by ethnic hatred, they tortured and slaughtered millions of Russians without a shred of human remorse. It cannot be overstated. Bolshevism committed the greatest human slaughter of all time. The fact that most of the world is ignorant and uncaring about this enormous crime is proof that the global media in the hands of the perpetrators. – Alexander Solzhenitsyn

If one wants to sum up *Two Hundred Years Together*, (Solzhenitsyn Book) it would be that Jews were behind the Bolshevist takeover of Russia, and Jews were, therefore, the people behind the murder of countless millions of Russians and other nationalities. This genocide may be considered the greatest one in all history, and yet, it is not talked about much in the media. The internment of Jews in National Socialist German camps, however, is discussed a lot in the media.

Under the Jewish-dominated government of the USSR (80% of the Bolsheviks were Jewish), an estimated 66 million Gentiles (non Jews) died at the hands of the Jewish minority that controlled the government, in between the years of 1918 and 1991, the period when the communists held sway in the Soviet Union.

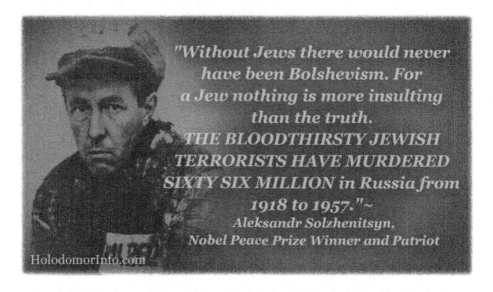

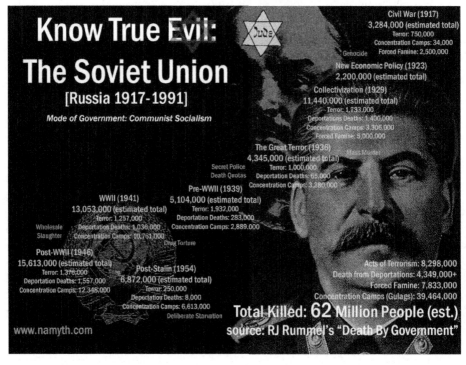

According to Solzhenitsyn, 66 million Soviets were killed by the state under the Bolsheviks. R.J. Rummel, who wrote *Death By Government* and coined the term "democide", estimates that 62 million USSR citizens, and others who fell under its jurisdiction, were murdered by the USSR government.

PRABHUPADA CONDEMNS JEWISH COMMUNISM

Guru-krpa: I've heard that in Russia the people are so eager to read imported literature that any literature appears they immediately buy it.

Prabhupada: Yes.

Tamala Krishna: There's a black market going on in Russia, particularly black market on books. Books are smuggled into the country and sold and they're very dearly read. People are very anxious.

Prabhupada: Yes. They must be because they are keeping in darkness.

Tamala Krishna: Yes.

Prabhupada: **These nasty countries, in the name of giving them material facility, they'll kill them, even they're independent. Such a horrible country. How people can tolerate loss of independence? It is very horrible.** I am sitting here 24 hours, this is another thing, but if I understand that I cannot go out, I have to sit down here, oh it is horrible. It is a horrible condition. Simply this impression that I have to keep myself within this room, although I am keeping myself, I am not going, only for walk maybe. But if the impression is that I cannot go out from this room, then my life is lost. This is psychology. So, they are keeping their young men. They are not allowed to go out of the country, in Russia. Similarly in China.

Tamala Krishna: Even more so.

Prabhupada: **So what kind of government it is? It is a horrible government.** And they are hackney only in literature. These communist country, the people are forced to accept the government regulation. And that is all bad. I have seen in Moscow, generally the people are morose, their face not very happy. They are also Europeans, they want freedom to go here and there (indistinct) and to work. The taxi driver--first of all there is scarcity of taxi, you cannot get taxi... *(Room Conversation, May 7, 1976, Honolulu)*

Prabhupada: Yes, everyone is in darkness. If you can make propaganda, the people will be misled. That is not very difficult. Just like from Russia, nobody is communist. But it is going on--

the Russia is communist country. I have studied thoroughly. Nobody is communist. Maybe a few only. But it is going on by propaganda that Russia is a communist country. The people in general, they are forced to accept it. **That book was written by some man, terrorism. It is terrorism. That's it. By force. Nobody accepts this communist philosophy, I have studied.** (everyone gets out of car) They were very, very unhappy. The young man cannot go out of the country. Just see. Restricted. How much uncomfortable he is feeling. Especially in European countries, the young men, they want to go. But they will not allow. They will not allow anything to read except Lenin's literature. What is this? Simply suppressing. Everyone is unhappy. Which way? This way? This is their position. I have seen it directly. And as soon as one is suspected that he is doing otherwise, he will be sent to some unknown camp. Nobody knows where he has gone.

Paramahamsa: Just like they had some people who came to Russia to start some Buddhist thing, and then they were sent away to some camp, concentration camp.

Prabhupada: Never seen again.

Paramahamsa: No one has seen them.

Prabhupada: Just see. This is their... **It is the most fallen country. No freedom. No freedom at all. Horrible country.**

Ganesa: Why don't the people revolt if they're so unhappy?

Prabhupada: Yes, they are revolting, but they are now so much suppressed they cannot... Sometimes there is revolt. Sometimes there is upheaval.

Paramahamsa: Not a big upheaval because they are terrorized. They are afraid that if they revolt, then they...

Prabhupada: **They will be killed.**

Paramahamsa: Yeah, the government will come out and just shoot them all.

Prabhupada: **Yes, all the Leninists and Stalinists, they kill. It is a country of terrorism. That's all. The government men, they are simply terrorists. That's all.**

Paramahamsa: Just like in Cambodia they just, the new Communist government, they executed tens and thousands of people just recently.

Prabhupada: Just see.

Paramahamsa: People who were working for the old government. They just killed them all. So this what the people are afraid of.

Prabhupada: **Yes. Terrorism. This Communism means terrorism.** (aside:) Thank you.

Amogha: I have a garland, but it's not finished. Almost...

Prabhupada: **Communism means terrorism. That I have seen. I have studied personally. By threat, by pressure, that's all. Nobody is communist in Russia.**

Jayadharma: Is the whole world going to become Communist, Prabhupada? Or is the whole world going to become Krishna cons...

Prabhupada: Nobody is Communist, but if the demons are powerful, they will declare.

Paramahamsa: They will introduce it.

Prabhupada: They will not introduce; they will declare like that, falsely. That's all.

(Morning Walk, May 8, 1975, Perth)

Ramesvara: Yes. But actually the Russians have so much cheated that...

Prabhupada: They must cheat, because they are first-class rogue.

Hari-sauri: Actually what's happened is that America has given away...

Prabhupada: I hesitate to say "they," (because) the Russian people are nice.

Hari-sauri: The Communist Party.

Prabhupada: **The Party is dangerous. I've studied the Russians. They are nice.**

Ramesvara: Victimized.

Prabhupada: **Yes, victimized. They have been suppressed by force, terrorism. Otherwise nice Russian people are as good as others. And they do not like this government. That's a fact.** But what can be done? They are forced to accept. Nobody is happy. Everyone is morose.

Hari-sauri: Yes. They're all afraid to speak.

Prabhupada: Yes. No freedom.

Ramesvara: No intellectual freedom.

Prabhupada: Yes.

Ramesvara: That's very well known.

Prabhupada: No, even physical. You cannot go out without government consent. And they don't allow, especially young men. They do not allow to go out of the country.

Ramesvara: No, I was reading to you that if they apply for leaving the country, then immediately there is a long delay.

Prabhupada: Yes.

Ramesvara: But during that delay they are forced to lose their job, so they have no income. Then people from outside Russia who are sympathizers start to send money, and the government takes sixty-five percent of it in taxes before the people can get it. So they torture them if they want to leave.

Prabhupada: **Yes. Terrorism. Very dangerous.** Now it is published in the paper how they exploit the people. And our India also thinking in terms of Russian philosophy. Lenin's philosophy.

Hari-sauri: They're not so successful here, though. The people are too pious to accept Communist philosophy so much here.

Prabhupada: Hm, yes. It will be difficult here.

(Conversation During Massage, January 23, 1977, Bhubaneswar)

Prabhupada: It will go on like that. In America (indistinct), why you are envious of me? That disease is there. His enviousness is a different quality. Actually, comparing with America, the people are more happy in America, not in Russia. It's a fact. I have seen it. **They are terrorized, no freedom. So everyone is terrorized, they must be. What is that? Is that life? I have to live under terrorism conditions. I must do it. (indistinct). It is not life.** *(Conversations 740911RC.VRN)*

In Russia, even if you are foreigner, they can immediately send you to the concen..., without any knowledge, they don't care for your embassy or your... **Such a rascal state, there is no civilized method.** They send their own men, such an important man like that Kruschev. He was sent into oblivion; nobody knows where he is. **Such a rascal government. Very difficult to live in. People are... Simply under terrorism the**

government is going on. In that sense your American government is so nice. Everyone has got the liberty. **What is that nonsense government--terrorism.** *(Prabhupada Garden Conversation, June 22, 1976, New Vrindaban)*

Paramahamsa: ksipamy ajasram asubhan asurisv eva yonisu "Those who are envious and mischievous, who are the lowest among men, are cast by Me into the ocean of material existence, into various demoniac species of life."

Prabhupada: **All of them are going to Russia to take birth. Yes.** **Not Russian people are bad. That is a mistake. Some of them. Some people are good. That I have experienced**. Otherwise how... (aside:) Don't do that. Otherwise how that Anatole came to become my...? And there are many like that, mostly like him. It is by artificial suppression that it has been advertised, "The Russian people are all Communist." **That's not fact. That's not fact. Simply some rogues and thieves and demons, by threats... It is a country of, what is called? Terrorism. A terror. People have decided to leave this country, but they cannot leave.** Mostly Russians, they want to leave that country, and some of them already done so. Many Russians have fled away. Many Chinese men have fled away. They don't like this philosophy.

Paramahamsa: Also the East Europe countries, Eastern Europe countries.

Prabhupada: Many countries. It is unnatural to deny God. It is unnatural. This is also Krishna's another magic. All such people who had any doubt about Krishna, they have been kept over there in Russia. Just like the other day there was a train crash accident. So all these rascals they are brought together in that way in a train or two train, and they smashed. That is... Just like Krishna did in Battle of Kuruksetra. All the rascals were brought into the battlefield and finished. *(Arrival Talk in Room, Mayapur, March 23, 1975)*

This last quote is very interesting, as Prabhupada is saying that the envious and mischievous, who are the lowest among men, have taken birth in Russia as the leaders. These are the demoniac subterranean alien race that wishes to rule the world under Godless tyranny. These demons have now taken control of all governments of the world and are now planning to massacre the remaining free people of the world, especially the Americans and Europeans. We are now on the verge of World War 3. WE PRAY THE LORD COMES AS AN INCARNATION AND LEADS THE PIOUS TO VICTORY AND RAINS DOWN TOTAL DESTRUCTION OVER THE DEMONS!!!!

Prabhupada's Letter to Sumati Morarji

New York, 27 October, 1965.

Madam Sumati Morarji Baisaheba,

Please accept my greetings. I am very glad to acknowledge receipt of your letter dated the 9th instant and have noted the contents. Since I have landed in U.S.A. I have improved in my health and I am very glad to see that in America practically everything is available for our Indian vegetarian dishes. By the grace of Lord Krishna the American are prosperous in every respect and they are not poverty stricken like the Indians. The people in general are satisfied so far their material needs are concerned and they are spiritually inclines. When I was in Butler, Pennsylvania about 500 miles from the New York city, I saw there many churches and they were attending regularly. This shows that they are spiritually inclines. I was also invited by some churches church governed schools and colleges and I spoke there and they appreciated and presented me some token rewards. When I was speaking to the students they were very much eagerly hearing me about the principles of Srimad-Bhagavatam rather the clergymen were cautious to allow the students to hear me so patiently. They thought that the students may not be converted into Hindu ideas as it is quite natural for any religious sect. But they do not know that the devotional service of the Lord (Sri Krishna) is the common religion for every one including the aborigines and the cannibals in the jungles.

Any way so far I have studied the American people they are very much eager to learn about the Indian way spiritual realisation and there are so many so called Yoga asramas in America. Unfortunately they are not very much adored by the Government and it is heard that such yoga asramas have exploited the innocent people as it has been the case in India also. The only hope is that they are spiritually inclined and immense benefit can be done to them if the Cult of Srimad-Bhagavatam is preached here.

The American public also give reception to the Indian art and music. So many of them come and every one of them is given good reception. Recently one dancer from Madras came here (Balasaraswati) and just to see the mode of reception, I went to see the dance with a friend although for the last forty years I have never attended such dance ceremony. The dancer was successful in her demonstration. The music was in Indian classical tune mostly in sanskrit language and the American public appreciated them. So I was encouraged to see the favorable circumstances about my future preaching work.

The Bhagavata cult is preached also through the art of music and dance as it was done by Lord Caitanya. I am just thinking of introducing the very same system for my Bhagavatam preaching but I have no means. The Christian missionary people are backed by huge resources and they preach the Christian cult all over the world. Similarly the devotees of Lord Krishna may also combine together to start the mission of preaching Bhagavatam cult all over the world. It is not for serving any political purpose but it is necessary to preach cult for saving the people in general from the dangerous tendency of Godlessness. The Christian cult or any other cult cannot save the people from being under the clutches of the growing communism but the Bhagavatam cult can save them because of its philosophical and scientific approach.

I am therefore thinking of bringing a Sankirtana party from India but I do not know how to do it. Unless there is an organized party or association it is very difficult to do it. The Rama Krishna Mission here is busy in preaching a misrepresentation and therefore practically they have failed to preach the real cult of India. The so called Yogis also could not establish the real cult of Bhagavad-gita. They are after material gains. The Bhagavata Cult is not there at all although it is the only remedy for raising the people in the world in the path of self realisation and spiritual salvation.

I do not know what is in the mind of Lord Bala Krishna but I think that your attention to give an impetus to the Bhagavata cult and my humble attempt can serve great purpose. By the grace of the Lord you have a great position in the world and it is learnt that you are one of the richest woman in the world. But above all you are a pious lady with great devotion for Lord Bala Krishna and you can do a lot in this connection.

By the Grace of Lord Bala Krishna you are also free from all family encumbrances and as I have see you in your Palm Ban house, you live like a sage and a Tapaswini. I wish that you may take up this idea of Bhagavatam preaching work a little more seriously. What I want that immediately a society for this purpose may be formed and that will be recognized by the Government for cultural activity. So many cultural missions come here from India at the expense of Government and they simply waste the money. But if there is a real cultural mission for preaching the Bhagavatam cult a great philanthropic work will be done for the human society at large. I am just giving you the idea and if you kindly think over the matter seriously and consult your beloved Lord Bala Krishna surely you will be further enlightened in the matter. There is scope and there is necessity also and it is the duty of every Indian specially the devotees of Lord Krishna to take up the matter.

I shall be glad to hear from you about my humble suggestions per return of mail. Hope you are well. With my best regards, I am

Yours sincerely,

A. C. Bhaktivedanta Swami.

N.B. I am very glad to note the last line of your letter under reply in which you write to say "I feel that if you should stay there till you fully recover from your illness and return only after you have completed your mission."

Yes I wish to stay here for all the days till I have finished the mission of life to preach Bhagavata Cult very rightly and for this very reason only I have suggested the above means and ways. If you kindly cooperate informing a society for this purpose with your great influence surely all Indians will combine and thus we can fulfill the mission very nicely declaring the glories of India. Please do it for the Lord's sake.

The Offensive Vaishnava Calendar

The following images are from the Vaishnava calendar of 2022. In the first picture you will clearly see on the 31st Halloween and on the 4th Yom Kippur. In the second picture you will see Hanukkah on the 18th. These are also present in the 2023 calendar.

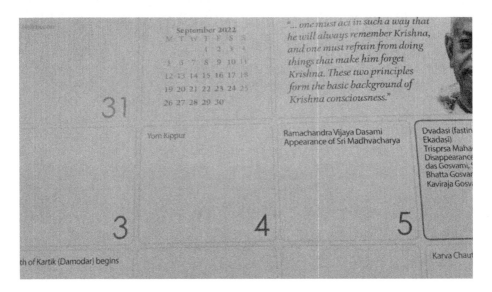

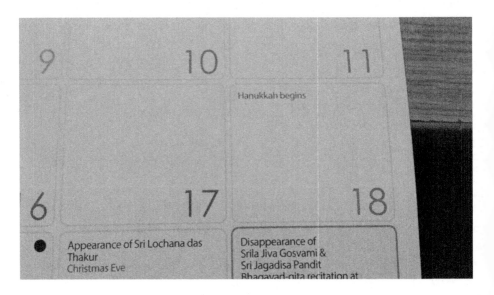

Not only is the transcendental Jaladuta pastime not worshipped by devotees in ISKCON but it isn't even mentioned in the Vaishnava calendar. Yet in the same calendar we will find Yom Kippur, Hanukkah and Halloween. These are totally demoniac rituals that have no place in a calendar for devotees of Krishna. The fact that they are in the calendar proves clearly that the great sinister movement now controls ISKCON.

Yom Kippur can be summarised as follows: Be a Jew > Sin all Year > Transfer your sins to a chicken > Torture the chicken and kill it > The chicken goes to hell instead of you > Yay! We fooled God.

Hanukkah: The Jews celebration of their brutal supremacy over the non-jews or goyim (human animals).

Halloween: A celebration of Jewish ritual child sacrifice.

Please check my video on this topic at the following link:

SATANIC YOM KIPPUR & HALLOWEEN CELEBRATED IN ISKCON CALENDAR – PROOF THE JEWS RUN THE CULT

https://truth.prabhupada.org.uk/satanic-yom-kippur-halloween-celebrated-in-iskcon-calender-proof-the-jews-run-the-cult

About The Author

I was first blessed with Prabhupada's association in 1988.

Even though I wasn't raised a Christian, I always remember appreciating Jesus Christ through my school years, especially during Bible based assemblies and Church visits.

When I was 20 years old and living alone in my flat, one day I picked up an old Bible from my book shelf and looked at the section of Jesus preaching his Sermon on the Mount. I read parts and remember thinking: "I would love to have been a real disciple of Jesus". The Lord in the heart noted my desire and shortly thereafter, He sent to me the Jesus Christ of our times, namely Srila Prabhupada.

ACCEPTING PRABHUPADA IN MY HEART

I accepted Srila Prabhupada in my heart the moment I saw his face on the book I received from a friend. I could immediately feel that here was a personality that I could fully trust. He didn't want anything from me but was simply coming to help me, to give me a message of profound truth.

My feelings were confirmed when I started to read Prabhupada's books. Here was a Divine Messenger from the Lord conveying the highest spiritual knowledge in a most easy-to-understand fashion. I was totally captivated!

I gradually developed my relationship with Prabhupada through hearing his lectures, chanting kirtans with him and reading his books. In a short period of time, I was chanting 16 rounds and I was determined to surrender and become a full time devotee in his ISKCON movement.

JOINING ISKCON

After giving away most of my belongings and selling my home, I went to live in a small temple in Birmingham. I was very disappointed to hear from the ISKCON leadership that Prabhupada was no longer available as the guru, but had instructed that all future devotees coming to his movement accept his advanced disciples as initiating spiritual masters and be guided by one of them.

I served for nearly four years in ISKCON mainly doing full time book distribution and also cooking. I approached various gurus but they could never compare to Prabhupada who had won my heart by his purity. In fact he saved me from surrendering to one of those rogues and nondevotees posing as a pure devotee by the following words he spoke to me:

> This is the first condition. First of all find out such person whom, upon whom you have full faith that whatever he will say, you will accept. That is guru. *[Prabhupada Lecture, Bhagavad-gita 13.1-2 Miami, February 26, 1975]*

I never had full faith in any of these men, thus I couldn't surrendered to them. Eventually by my prayers, Krishna sent me a real disciple of Prabhupada who helped me understand that rotten smell that lingered in ISKCON, that thing that just didn't seem right. After preaching the truth about Prabhupada being the only diksa guru for ISKCON, I was quickly banned from the movement.

GOING BACK TO THE START

Thus I returned to my former position of taking direct shelter of Prabhupada as I had done before my ISKCON experience. I was like a withered flower that was blessed and drenched from the heavens by the mercy of the rain clouds. I regained my intelligence and enthusiasm. I regained my very life!

I was now very determined that I would never be deceived again. I made it my mission that I would hear every lecture and conversation Prabhupada ever gave. I would read all his books. No rascal would push his concoctions past me ever again!

MEETING SULOCANA DASA THE
PERFECT DISCIPLE & THE LILAMRTA

During this period, around 1993, I read The Guru Business by Sulocana prabhu. This book had a powerful effect on me. "Here was a true disciple of Prabhupada who gave his life to expose the deceivers and re-establish Prabhupada's true mission" I thought. I was deeply impressed by his example and powerful message.

The most powerful instruction I received from Sulocana prabhu was the following:

> "He left us his own autobiography, as it is." *(Sulocana dasa,*
> *Guru Business Preface – A Rude Awakening)*

These words were implanted in my heart by Prabhupada's perfect disciple, and eventually manifested in November of 2001, as the wonderful autobiography of His Divine Grace called "Srila Prabhupada Lilamrta As It Is".

So from 1993 as I was hearing Prabhupada constantly, I was collecting all the beautiful words from his lotus mouth about his life, character and qualities. These formed the basis of the book. I also printed The Guru Business as a photocopy booklet.

ALL OF US SHOULD HEAR PRABHUPADA

Along with this I decided that I should also compile a book of Prabhupada's quotes about the importance of hearing from the pure devotee. From my own experience I was seeing that hearing from Prabhupada was giving me back my life which was gradually fading away in the ISKCON cult. I knew that if others would take to this process then the original mission of Prabhupada could be revived. I named the book "All Of Us Should Hear Prabhupada". It was printed in late 1993.

We must admit that we have realized definitely that the divine message from his holy lips is the congenial thing for suffering humanity. All of us should hear him patiently. If we listen to the transcendental sound without unnecessary opposition, he will surely have mercy upon us. The Acarya's Message is to take us back to our original home, back to God. Let me repeat, therefore, that we should hear him patiently, follow him in the measure of our conviction, and bow down at his lotus feet for releasing us from our present causeless unwillingness for serving the Absolute and all souls.

(Srila Prabhupada's Vyasa Puja offering, 1936)

A PRABHUPADA TEMPLE

Shortly after this I managed to open a small preaching temple in the UK where Prabhupada was worshiped as the initiating guru. The temple was based on the principle that Prabhupada's vibration remained playing 24 hours a day in the building and he would give the morning and evening classes. Devotees would also experience the bliss of chanting in kirtan with Prabhupada leading the chanting.

PRABHUPADA ON YOUTUBE

In 2005 I was one of the first people to put Prabhupada's videos on YouTube. Prabhupada gave me the good preaching intelligence to tag the Illuminati in the titles of the videos. This had an amazing effect and one of the videos had around 1.2 million views and a few others half a million views. Later my channel was hacked and all videos deleted. Still many people became devotees from associating directly with Prabhupada during that period.

PRABHUPADA BULLOCK CART IN VRINDAVAN 2007/08

As you may already know, in November 1977 at Krishna Balarama Mandir, Vrindavan, Srila Prabhupada repeatedly requested to be released from his room in which he was locked by Ravana disciples. His Divine Grace desired that his real disciples and sincere servants break free from the influence of these Ravana disciples and thwart their sinister plan to poison him, by taking him from the room for Bullock Cart Tirthasthana.

During the Kartik months of 2007 and 2008, which was the 30th anniversary of Prabhupada's disappearance, I went to Vrindavan with my family and a few friends and we executed Prabhupada's REAL FINAL ORDER by taking him on Bullock Cart Parikrama in Vrndavana. Prabhupada led the LOUD chanting and it was SIMPLY ECSTATIC!!!

We were all instrumental in releasing this brahmastra of Prabhupada's Love of Godhead from Vrindavan Dhama at Kartik, penetrating the universal shell and cracking the hearts of the demons!!! The strength of the modern day Kamsa demons [International Jewry] who are trying to rule the world without God was curbed down or curtailed by this sacrifice of LOUD PRABHUPADA SANKIRTANA!!! (See Srimad Bhagavatam 1.1.4)

GIVING PRABHUPADA TO THE JEW PILLED

I was always aware of the favourable things Prabhupada said about Hitler. In 2015 after watching "Adolf Hitler The Greatest Story NEVER Told", I started to understand more deeply the essential service Hitler did to protect the west from the Godless Jewish Bolsheviks, thus allowing the message of Prabhupada to be imparted there to begin an Aryan resurrection.

It was then very clear to me that those people who were awakened to the Jewish problem are the best recipients for the spiritual truths that Prabhupada is giving. This is a big topic that I will cover in my next book called "THE FIGHT FOR MOTHER EARTH - Communism Against Krishna Consciousness For The Soul Of Man". This has been the focus of my preaching work in this last period. Bringing all those Jew pilled souls to the lotus feet of Prabhupada. Or as Hitler called him: "The One, The Man to Come, The New Messiah".

THE GURU BUSINESS & KILLING FOR KEITH

Recently with the publication of his book called "Killing For Krishna", Henry Doktorski, the deranged follower of Keith Ham (aka Kirtanananda), has viciously attacked Prabhupada's perfect disciple Sulocana prabhu.

This attack by Doktorski has been the catalyst for me to get Sulocana's Guru Business professionally published for the first time. I had previously printed it twice before as a photocopy booklet after reading it in 1993, and later around 1998, but the illusory energy of the Lord was always checking my desire to print it as a beautiful book befitting its glorious stature. Now I am truly proud and honoured to have been given the service of getting The Guru Business into print, at long last!!!

If anyone actually reads this printing of Sulocana's Guru Business, that in and of itself, will destroy the slanderous mental speculations presented by Henry Doktorski in his book "Killing For Krishna". Still as a follower of Sulocana, I cannot sit idly and allow this deranged rogue and nondevotee to blaspheme Prabhupada's perfect disciple. As silence means acceptance!!! THUS I HAVE DEFENDED THE HONOR OF SULOCANA PRABHU AND EXPOSED THE BLASPHEMER HENRY DOKTORSKI WITH MY BOOK KILLING FOR KEITH.

PRABHUPADA AND THE JALADUTA INCARNATIONS

In this year of 2023, I have been blessed to complete a new book about Srila Prabhupada. The main purpose for compiling this book is to establish in the devotee community of the whole world, worship of Srila Prabhupada and the Jaladuta Incarnations. This transcendental pastime should be celebrated as a yearly festival by all devotees of the Lord.

This divine lila of Srila Prabhupada with the Lord reveals to us very clearly the exalted personality of His Divine Grace and the importance of his great mission of spreading love of Krishna to all the fallen conditioned souls.

Prabhupada's position in the ten thousand year Golden Age now unfolding on this planet is so pivotal that the Lord personally incarnated in multiple transcendental forms to protect and carry him on the Jaladuta to America.

Other Books Available

Śrīla Prabhupāda
Līlāmṛta As It Is

The Pastimes of His Divine Grace
A.C. Bhaktivedanta Swami Prabhupāda

Prabhupada's Authorized Autobiography

SRILA PRABHUPADA LILAMRTA AS IT IS - Mukunda dasa

The Pastimes of His Divine Grace

A.C. Bhaktivedanta Swami Prabhupada

First Printing 2001

"Srila Prabhupada speaks out. He speaks for himself about himself. Truly a work of pure love and devotion. Fully utilizing all the space on every page to print the actual words spoken by Srila Prabhupada himself about the mission of his life to spread Krsna-consciousness all over the world." Krsna dasa, India.

Hear the life story of His Divine Grace A.C. Bhaktivedanta Swami Prabhupada directly from his own lotus mouth that is authentic!

"If you want to know me, then you must know about me from me. You can not speculate about me." [Srila Prabhupada Room Conversation with Reporter June 4, 1976, Los Angeles] "So that means, anyway, if you want to know about me, then you must know from me. That is authentic. That is authentic." [Srila Prabhupada from a Bhagavad-gita Lecture, 3.17-20, New York, May 27, 1966]

ALL OF US SHOULD HEAR PRABHUPADA - Mukunda dasa

First Printing 1993 - Second Printing 1999.

This book is a compilation of quotes from the teachings of HIS DIVINE GRACE A.C. BHAKTIVEDANTA SWAMI PRABHUPADA on the importance of hearing from a self realized soul. The simple practice of hearing Srila Prabhupada lecture twice daily in association puts His Divine Grace practically in the center of all our lives. By hearing from Srila Prabhupada all misconceptions will be cleansed from our hearts. Then we can unite and spread the Sankirtana Movement in every town and village in the world.

"Every devotee who follows Prabhupada's teachings should have this book!" - Rukmini Devi Dasi (USA)

We have recently published the Guru Business by Sulocana Prabhu. This is the first time it has been printed in a professional format. The book is very beautifully presented in soft back with 420 pages and 12 colour plates. This powerful book of truth will be so much beneficial for the devotee community and public at large.

"Anyone who has read The Guru Business will have at once felt the powerful and illuminating clarity in the words of Sulocana prabhu. The way in which he has strung Prabhupada's words together, like pearls on the thread of his own amazing realizations, came from his total surrender to the instruction of Srila Prabhupada. Sulocana prabhu was prepared to die rather than not execute Prabhupada's mission properly. Because of this faith not only did the Lord manifest Prabhupada's previously hidden letters to Sulocana but he revealed their purport in his heart." Mukunda dasa from Killing For Keith, Chapter Seven.

NEW PRINTING!!! "Henry Doktorski's recent book called Killing For Krishna, The Danger Of Deranged Devotion, falls in the same category as ISKCON's biography of Srila Prabhupada. It is an offensive book of poisonous slander that is nicely sugar coated with false glorification, so that the foolish will swallow it and thus commit spiritual suicide. The only difference between the two books is that Killing For Krishna lacks any of the subtleness of ISKCON's biography. Doktorski's slander of Sulocana is totally gross and in your face, unlike Satsvarupa's slander of Prabhupada which has a more covert nature. The amazing thing is that so many "devotees" claiming to be Prabhupada followers praise this offensive book that slanders Sulocana on page after page!" (Mukunda dasa - Killing For Keith, Chapter One)

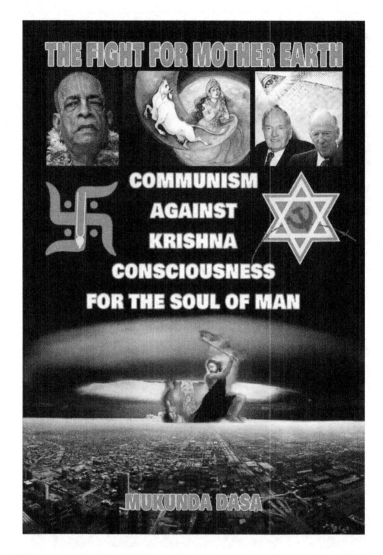

THIS BOOK WILL BE AVAILABLE SOON!!! "The fight between the Lord, the Supreme Personality of Godhead, and the demon is compared to a fight between bulls for the sake of a cow. The earth planet is also called go, or cow. As bulls fight between themselves to ascertain who will have union with a cow, there is always a constant fight between the demons and the Supreme Lord or His representative for supremacy over the earth." (Srila Prabhupada from Srimad Bhagavatam 3.18.20)

ALL THESE BOOKS CAN BE PURCHASE FROM PRABHUPADA STORE ON THE FOLLOWING LINK: https://www.gokula-incense.co.uk/ prabhupada-original-books-107-c.asp

Acknowledgements

Again I would like to thank my wife Gauri Devi Dasi for patiently helping me with all the editing and proof reading that had to be done to produce this book.

Also a special thanks to my daughter Vrindavani Devi Dasi who transcribed many of my videos that are presented in this book.

Hare Krishna. Jaya Prabhupada. Jaya Sulocana Prabhu.

Mukunda dasa

Printed in Great Britain
by Amazon

22369026R10130